95TH CONGRESS }
1st Session } HOUSE OF REPRESENTATIVES { DOCUMENT
No. 95-259

How Our Laws Are Made

By DR. CHARLES J. ZIN*

Revised and Updated

By

EDWARD F. WILLETT, JR., ESQ.

Law Revision Counsel

United States House of Representatives

PRESENTED BY MR. RODINO

November 3, 1977.—Ordered to be printed

UNITED STATES
GOVERNMENT PRINTING OFFICE
98-587 O   WASHINGTON : 1978

H. Con. Res. 190 [By Mr. Rodino] Passed November 3, 1977

NINETY-FIFTH CONGRESS OF THE UNITED STATES OF AMERICA
AT THE FIRST SESSION

*Begun and held at the City of Washington on Tuesday, the fourth
day of January, one thousand nine hundred and seventy-seven*

Concurrent Resolution

Resolved by the House of Representatives (the Senate concurring),
That the brochure entitled "How Our Laws Are Made", as set out in
House Document Numbered 94–509 of the Ninety-fourth Congress, be
printed as a House document, with a suitable paperback cover of a
style, design, and color, to be selected by the chairman of the Committee on the Judiciary of the House of Representatives, with emendations, and with a foreword by the Honorable Peter W. Rodino, Junior;
and that there be printed two hundred and forty-six thousand additional copies, of which twenty-five thousand shall be for the use of
the Committee on the Judiciary and the balance prorated to the Members of the House of Representatives.

SEC. 2. There shall be printed for the use of the Senate thirty-six
thousand four hundred additional copies of the document specified
in section 1 of this concurrent resolution.

Attest:

EDMUND L. HENSHAW, JR.,
Clerk of the House of Representatives.

Attest:

J. S. KIMMITT,
Secretary of the Senate.

(II)

EARLIER PRINTINGS

FOREWORD

By Hon. Peter W. Rodino, Jr., Chairman, Committee on the Judiciary of the House of Representatives

The framers of the United States Constitution, with unparalleled foresight, embodied in our system of Government the principle of "separation of powers," by establishing three equal and independent branches of Government—the Legislative, Executive, and Judicial.

The very first provision of the Constitution of the United States (Article I, Section 1) creates the Legislative Branch by providing that "All legislative Powers herein granted shall be vested in a Congress of the United States, which shall consist of a Senate and House of Representatives."

The Federal legislative process, which has developed as a result of this constitutional mandate, is extremely complex. Therefore, it is necessary for the American people to have access to documents and materials which will enable them to achieve a greater understanding and appreciation of this legislative process.

This need was recognized over twenty years ago by the late Dr. Charles J. Zinn, then Law Revision Counsel for the Committee on the Judiciary, when the first printing of "How Our Laws Are Made" was authorized in 1953.

Since that time this House Document has been widely distributed not only in the United States, but around the world. In addition, it has been translated and published in eight different languages and is frequently used as a model for similar governmental publications in many foreign countries. The pamphlet furthermore continues to be a valuable source material for classroom study and discussion throughout the United States.

Today, as much as anytime in our American history, the process of our American government is extremely important to all of us. The better we understand our government the better we can serve it and the better our government can serve us.

This edition was revised and updated by the Law Revision Counsel of the House of Representatives to reflect changes in the legislative procedure brought about by legislation and changes in the rules of the House of Representatives since the last edition.

It is my sincere hope that this pamphlet will be helpful and informative to all persons interested in how our laws are made.

November 3, 1977

CONTENTS

APPENDIX

FIGURES

HOW OUR LAWS ARE MADE

I. INTRODUCTION

This handbook is intended to provide a readable and nontechnical outline of the background and the numerous steps of our Federal lawmaking process from the origin of an idea for a legislative proposal through its publication as a statute. This is a matter about which the average citizen should be well informed so that he may be able to understand the everyday news reports and discussions concerning the work of Congress.

It is hoped that this handbook will enable the average citizen to gain a greater understanding of the Federal legislative process and its role as one of the bulwarks of our representative system. One of the most practical safeguards of the American democratic way of life is this legislative process that, with its emphasis on the protection of the minority, gives ample opportunity to all sides to be heard and make their views known. The fact that a proposal cannot become a law without consideration and approval by both Houses of Congress is an outstanding virtue of our legislative system. Open and full discussion provided for under our Constitution frequently results in the notable improvement of a bill by amendment before it becomes law, or the defeat of a bad proposal.

Because the large majority of laws originate in the House of Representatives, this discussion will be directed principally to the procedure in that body.

(1)

II. THE CONGRESS

Article I, section 1, of the United States Constitution, provides that—

All legislative Powers herein granted shall be vested in a Congress of the United States, which shall consist of a Senate and House of Representatives.

The Senate is composed of 100 Members—two from each State, irrespective of population or area—elected by the people in conformity with the provisions of the 17th Amendment to the Constitution. That amendment changed the former Constitutional method under which Senators were chosen by the respective State legislatures. A Senator must be at least 30 years of age, and have been a citizen of the United States for nine years and, when elected, a resident of the State for which he is chosen. The term of office is six years and one-third of the total membership is elected every second year. The terms of both Senators from a particular State are so arranged that they do not terminate at the same time. Of the two Senators from a State serving at the same time the one who was elected first—or if both were elected at the same time, the one elected for a full term—is referred to as the "senior" Senator from that State. The other is referred to as the "junior" Senator. The Constitution further provides that, in case of the death or resignation of a Senator during his term, the governor of the State must call a special election unless the State legislature has authorized him to appoint a successor until the next election, at which time a successor is elected for the balance of the term. Most of the State legislatures have granted their governors the power of appointment.

Each Senator has one vote.

As constituted in 1977—the 95th Congress—the House of Representatives is composed of 435 Members elected every two years from among the 50 States, apportioned to their total populations. The permanent number of 435 was established following the Thirteenth Decennial Census in 1910, as directed in article I, section 2, of the Constitution, and was increased temporarily to 437 for the 87th Congress, to provide for one Member each for Alaska and Hawaii. It seems undesirable to make a considerable increase in the number of Members, because a larger body, similar to the British House of Commons, consisting of 630 members, would be too unwieldy. The Constitution limits the number of Representatives to not more than one for every 30,000 of population, and, under a former apportionment in one State a particular Member represented more than 900,000 constituents, while another in the same State was elected from a district having a population of only 175,000. The Supreme Court [1] has since held unconstitutional a Missouri statute permitting a maximum population variance of 3.1 percent from mathematical equality. The Court said that the variances among the districts were not unavoidable and,

---

[1] *Kirkpatrick* v. *Preisler*, 394 U.S. 526.

therefore, were invalid. This is an interpretation of the Court's earlier decision that "as nearly as is practicable one man's vote in a Congressional election is to be worth as much as another's".

A law enacted in 1967 has abolished all "at-large" elections (i.e., Members elected by the voters of the entire State rather than in a Congressional district within the State) except, of course, in States entitled to only one Representative. (2 U.S.C. § 2c)

A Representative must be at least 25 years of age and have been a citizen of the United States for seven years and, when elected, a resident of the State in which he is chosen. In case of the death or resignation of a Member during his term, the governor of his State may call a special election for the choosing of a successor to serve for the unexpired portion of the term.

Each Representative has one vote.

In addition to the Representatives from 50 States, there is a Resident Commissioner from the Commonwealth of Puerto Rico, as authorized by an act of 1917 (48 U.S.C. § 891) and in 1970 the Congress by Pub. L. 91-405 (D.C. Code, § 1-291), created the office of Delegate to the House of Representatives from the District of Columbia. In 1972 the Congress by Pub. L. 92-271 (48 U.S.C. § 1711), granted nonvoting Delegate representation to the territories of Guam and the Virgin Islands, as well. The Resident Commissioner and the Delegates have most of the prerogatives of Representatives, with the important exception of the right to vote on matters before the House.

Under the provisions of section 2 of the 20th amendment to the Constitution, Congress must assemble at least once every year, at noon on the 3d day of January, unless by law they appoint a different day.

A Congress lasts for two years, commencing in January of the year following the biennial election of Members, and is divided into two sessions.

Unlike some other parliamentary bodies, both the Senate and the House of Representatives have equal legislative functions and powers (except that only the House of Representatives may initiate revenue bills), and the designation of one as the "upper" House and the other as the "lower" House is not appropriate.

The Constitution authorizes each House to determine the rules of its proceedings. Pursuant to that authority the House of Representatives adopts its rules on the opening day of each Congress. The Senate operates under its rules adopted in 1884 and amended from time to time since then.

The chief function of the Congress is the making of laws. In addition, the Senate has the function of advising and consenting to treaties and to certain nominations by the President. In the matter of impeachments, the House of Representatives presents the charges—a function similar to that of grand juries—and the Senate sits as a court to try the impeachment. Both Houses meet in joint session on January 6th, following a presidential election, to count the electoral votes. (3 U.S.C. § 15) If no candidate receives a majority of the total electoral votes, the House of Representatives chooses the President from among the three candidates having the largest number of votes, and the Senate chooses the Vice President from the two candidates having the largest number of votes for that office.

III. SOURCES OF LEGISLATION

Sources of ideas for legislation are unlimited, and proposed drafts of bills originate in many diverse quarters. First of these is, of course the idea and draft conceived by a Member himself. This may emanate from his election campaign during which he had promised to introduce legislation on a particular subject, if elected. His entire campaign may have been based upon one or more such proposals. Or, through his experience after taking office he may have become aware of the need for amendment or repeal of existing laws or the enactment of a statute in an entirely new field.

In addition, his constituents—either as individuals or by corporate activity such as citizen groups or associations, bar associations, labor unions, manufacturers' associations, and chambers of commerce—may avail themselves of the right to petition, which is guaranteed by the First Amendment to the Constitution, and transmit their proposals to him. Many excellent laws have originated in this way since some of those organizations, because of their vital concern with various areas of legislation, have considerable knowledge regarding the laws affecting their interests and have the services of expert legislative draftsmen at their disposal for this purpose. If the Member is favorably impressed by the idea he may introduce the proposal in the form in which it has been submitted to him or he may first redraft it. In all events he may consult with the Legislative Counsel of the House or the Senate, as the case may be, to frame the ideas in suitable legislative language and form for introduction.

In modern times the "executive communication" has become a prolific source of legislative proposals. This is usually in the form of a letter from a member of the President's Cabinet or the head of an independent agency—or even from the President himself—transmitting a draft of a proposed bill to the Speaker of the House of Representatives and the President of the Senate. Despite the system of separation of powers, section 3 of article II of the Constitution imposes an obligation on the President to report to the Congress from time to time on the state of the Union and to recommend for consideration such measures as he considers necessary and expedient. Many of these executive communications follow on the President's message on the state of the Union delivered to the Congress in accordance with the mandate set out in section 3 of article II of the Constitution. The communication is then referred to the standing committee having jurisdiction of the subject matter embraced in the proposal since a bill may be introduced only by a Member of Congress. The chairman of that committee usually introduces the bill promptly either in the form in which it was received or with changes he considers necessary or desirable. This practice prevails even when the majority of the House and the President are not of the same political party, although there is no constitutional or statutory requirement that a bill be introduced to effectuate the recommendations. Otherwise, the message may be considered by the committee or one of its subcommittees to determine whether a bill should be introduced. The most important of the regular executive communications is the annual message from the President transmitting the proposed budget to the Congress. This, together with testimony by officials of the various branches of the Government before the Appropriations Committees of the House and Senate, is the basis of the several appropriation bills that are drafted by the House Committee on Appropriations.

Several of the executive departments and independent agencies have staffs of trained legislative counsels whose functions include the drafting of bills to be forwarded to the Congress with a request for their enactment.

The drafting of statutes is an art that requires great skill, knowledge, and experience. In some instances a draft is the result of a study covering a period of a year or more by a commission or committee designated by the President or one of his Cabinet officers. The Administrative Procedure Act and the Uniform Code of Military Justice are only two of many examples of enactments resulting from such studies. In addition, Congressional committees sometimes draft bills after studies and hearings covering periods of a year or more. Bills to codify the laws relating to crimes and criminal procedure, the judiciary and judicial procedure, the Armed Forces, and other subjects, have each required several years of preparation.

IV. FORMS OF CONGRESSIONAL ACTION

The work of the Congress is initiated by the introduction of a proposal in one of four principal forms. These are: the bill, the joint resolution, the concurrent resolution, and the simple resolution. By far the most customary form used in both Houses is the bill. During the 94th Congress (1975–1976), there were introduced in both Houses, more than 19,760 bills and 1,330 joint resolutions. Of this number 15,863 bills and 1,119 joint resolutions originated in the House of Representatives.

For the sake of simplicity this discussion will be confined generally to the procedure on a House of Representatives bill, but a brief comment will be made about each of the forms.

BILLS

A bill is the form used for most legislation, whether permanent or temporary, general or special, public or private.

The House of Representatives Manual prescribes the form of a House bill, as follows:

A BILL

For the establishment, etc. [as the title may be].

Be it enacted by the Senate and House of Representatives of the United States of America in Congress assembled, That, etc.

The enacting clause was prescribed by law in 1871 and is identical in all bills, whether they originate in the House of Representatives or in the Senate.

Bills may originate in either the House of Representatives or the Senate, with one notable exception provided for by the Constitution. Article I, section 7, of the Constitution, provides that all bills for raising revenue shall originate in the House of Representatives but the Senate may propose or concur with amendments, as on other bills. General appropriation bills also originate in the House of Representatives.

Article I, section 8, prescribes the matters concerning which the Congress may legislate, while section 9 of the same article places certain limitations upon Congressional action.

A bill originating in the House of Representatives is designated by the letters "H.R." followed by a number that it retains throughout all its parliamentary stages. The letters signify "House of Representatives" and not, as is sometimes supposed, "House resolution". A Senate bill is designated by the letter "S." followed by its number.

A bill that has been agreed to in identical form by both bodies becomes the law of the land only after—

    (1) Presidential approval; or

(2) failure by the President to return it with his objections to the House in which it originated within 10 days while the Congress is in session; (See Fig. 11, p. 68) or

(3) the overriding of a Presidential veto by a two-thirds vote in each House. (See Fig. 12, p. 69.)

It does not become law without the President's signature if the Congress by their adjournment prevent its return with his objections. This is known as a "pocket veto".

JOINT RESOLUTIONS

Joint resolutions may originate either in the House of Representatives or in the Senate—not, as may be supposed, jointly in both Houses. There is little practical difference between a bill and a joint resolution and, although the latter are not as numerous as bills, the two forms are often used indiscriminately. Statutes that have been initiated as bills have later been amended by a joint resolution, and vice versa. Both are subject to the same procedure—with the exception of joint resolutions proposing an amendment to the Constitution that must be approved by two-thirds of both Houses and are then sent directly to the Administrator of General Services for submission to the several States for ratification, and that are not presented to the President for his approval.

The form of a House joint resolution is prescribed by the House of Representatives Manual, as follows:

JOINT RESOLUTION

. Authorizing etc. [as the title may be].

Resolved by the Senate and House of Representatives of the United States of America in Congress assembled, That all, etc.

The resolving clause is identical in both House and Senate joint resolutions, having been prescribed by statute in 1871. It is frequently preceded by one or more "whereas" clauses indicating the necessity for or the desirability of the joint resolution.

The term "joint" does not signify simultaneous introduction and consideration in both Houses.

A joint resolution originating in the House of Representatives is designated "H.J. Res." followed by its individual number which it retains throughout all its parliamentary stages. One originating in the Senate is designated "S.J. Res." followed by its number.

Joint resolutions become law in the same manner as bills.

CONCURRENT RESOLUTIONS

Matters affecting the operations of both Houses are usually initiated by means of concurrent resolutions. These are not normally legislative in character but are used merely for expressing facts, principles, opinions, and purposes of the two Houses. They are not equivalent to a bill and their use is narrowly limited within these bounds.

The term "concurrent" does not signify simultaneous introduction and consideration in both Houses.

A concurrent resolution originating in the House of Representatives is designated "H. Con. Res." followed by its individual number, while a Senate concurrent resolution is designated "S. Con. Res." together with its number. On approval by both Houses they are signed by the Clerk of the House and the Secretary of the Senate and transmitted to the Administrator of General Services for publication in a special part of the Statutes at Large. They are not presented to the President for action as in the cases of bills and joint resolutions unless they contain a proposition of legislation, that, of course, is not within their scope in their modern form.

SIMPLE RESOLUTIONS

A matter concerning the operation of either House alone is initiated by a simple resolution. A resolution affecting the House of Representatives is designated "H. Res." followed by its number, while a Senate resolution is designated "S. Res." together with its number. They are considered only by the body in which they were introduced and on adoption are attested to by the Clerk of the House of Representatives or the Secretary of the Senate, as the case may be, and are published in the Congressional Record.

V. INTRODUCTION AND REFERENCE TO COMMITTEE

Any Member, the Resident Commissioner and the Delegates in the House of Representatives may introduce a bill at any time while the House is actually sitting by simply placing it in the "hopper" provided for the purpose at the side of the Clerk's desk in the House Chamber. He is not required to ask permission to introduce the measure or to make a statement at the time of introduction. Printed blank forms for use in typing the original bill are supplied through the stationery room. The name of the sponsor is endorsed on the bill. A public bill may be sponsored by up to 25 Members. To forestall the possibility that a bill might be introduced in the House on behalf of a Member without that Member's prior approval, the sponsoring Member's signature must appear on the bill before it is accepted for introduction. In the case where there are multiple sponsors of a bill, the signature must be that of the Member first named thereon. (See Speaker's directive, Congressional Record, Feb. 3, 1972, Vol. 118, Pt. 3, page 2521.) In the Senate, unlimited multiple sponsorship of a bill is permitted. Occasionally a Member may insert the words "by request" after his name to indicate that the introduction of the measure is in compliance with the suggestion of some other person.

The procedure is somewhat more formal in the Senate as governed by the standing rules of that body. At the time reserved for the purpose, a Senator who wishes to introduce a measure rises and states that he offers a bill for introduction, and sends it by page to the Secretary's desk. If objection is offered by any Senator the introduction is postponed until the next day. If there is no objection the bill is read by title for the first and second reading. Frequently, Senators obtain consent to have the bill printed at that point in the body of the Congressional Record, following their formal statement.

In the House of Representatives it is no longer the custom to read bills—even by title—at the time of introduction. The title is entered in the Journal and printed in the Congressional Record, thus preserving the purpose of the old rule. The bill is assigned its legislative number by the Clerk and referred to the appropriate committees by the Speaker (the Member elected to be the presiding Officer of the House) with the assistance of the Parliamentarian. These details appear in the daily issue of the Congressional Record. It is then sent to the Government Printing Office where it is printed in its introduced form, and printed copies are available shortly thereafter in the document rooms of both Houses. (See Fig. 1, p. 53.)

One copy is sent to the office of the chairman of the committee to which it has been referred, for action by that committee.

Perhaps the most important phase of the Congressional process is the action by committees. That is where the most intensive considera-

98-587 O - 78 - 3

tion is given to the proposed measures and where the people are given their opportunity to be heard. Nevertheless, this phase where such a tremendous volume of hard work is done by the Members is sometimes overlooked by the public, particularly when complaining about delays in enacting laws.

The Legislative Reorganization Acts of 1946 and 1970, the result of widespread proposals for "streamlining" Congress, establish the existing committee structure of the House and the Senate. Prior to the Reorganization Act of 1946, the House had 48 standing (permanent) committees and there were 33 in the Senate. In addition there were a number of select or special committees, usually of an investigative character, that normally did not consider pending legislation. There are, at present, 22 standing committees in the House and 15 in the Senate, as well as several select committees. In addition, there are several standing joint committees of the two Houses, two of which are the Joint Committee on Taxation and the Joint Economic Committee. Both Houses recently have made major changes in their committee organization. In 1974, the House adopted amendments to its rules that altered the jurisdiction and certain procedures of committees. In 1977, the Senate amended its rules to change the name, jurisdiction and size of certain committees, and reduced the number of standing committees from 18 to the present number, 15.

Each committee has jurisdiction over certain subject matters of legislation and all measures affecting a particular area of the law are referred to that committeee that has jurisdiction over it. For example, the Committee on the Judiciary has jurisdiction over measures relating to judicial proceedings, civil and criminal, generally, and 18 other categories, of which Constitutional amendments, revision and codification of statutes, civil liberties, antitrust, patents, copyrights and trademarks, are but a few. In all, the rules provide for 220 different classifications of measures that are to be referred to the respective committees in the House and 200 in the Senate. Membership on the various committees is divided between the two major political parties in proportion to their total membership in the House, except that one-half of the Members on the Committee on Standards of Official Conduct are from the majority party and one-half from the minority party. Until 1953, with the exception of the Members serving on the Committee on the District of Columbia, the former Committees on Un-American Activities and on Expenditures in the Executive Departments, or the Committee on House Administration, a Member could not serve on more than one standing committee of the House. This limitation was removed in January 1953, and now all Members may serve on more than one committee. In January 1971, the majority party of the House determined in caucus that (1) the chairman of a full committee may not be the chairman of more than one subcommittee of that committee, (2) a Member may not be chairman of more than one legislative subcommittee, and (3) a Member may not serve on more than two committees having legislative jurisdiction. These limitations do not apply to committees performing housekeeping functions and joint committees.

A Member usually seeks election to the committee that has jurisdiction over a field in which he is most qualified and interested. For example, the Committee on the Judiciary is composed entirely of lawyers. Many Members are nationally recognized experts in the specialty of their particular committee or subcommittee.

Members rank in seniority in accordance with the order of their appointment to the committee, and until recently the ranking majority Member was elected chairman. In 1975, the House amended its rules to require that committee chairmen be elected from nominations submitted by the majority party caucus.

Most of the committees have two or more subcommittees that, in addition to having general jurisdiction, specialize in the consideration of particular classifications of bills. Each standing committee of the House, except the Committee on the Budget, that has more than 20 members must establish at least four subcommittees.

Each committee is provided with a professional and clerical staff to assist it in the innumerable administrative details and other problems involved in the consideration of bills. For the standing committees, the professional staff (consisting of not more than eighteen, six of whom may be selected by the minority) is appointed on a permanent basis solely on the basis of fitness to perform the duties of their respective positions. The clerical staff (consisting of not more than twelve, four of whom may be selected by the minority) is appointed to handle correspondence and stenographic work for the committee staff and the chairman and ranking minority Member on matters related to committee work. All staff appointments are made by a majority vote of the committee without regard to race, creed, sex or age. The minority staff provisions do not apply to the Committee on Standards of Official Conduct because of its bipartisan nature. The Committee on Appropriations and the Committee on the Budget have special authority under the House rules for appointment of staff and assistants for the minority.

Under certain conditions a standing committee may appoint consultants on a temporary or intermittent basis and may also provide financial assistance to members of its professional staff for the purpose of acquiring specialized training, whenever the committee determines that such training will aid the committee in the discharge of its responsibilities.

VI. CONSIDERATION BY COMMITTEE

The chairman of the committee to which a bill has been referred may, on his own initiative, or at the request of the sponsor, refer the bill to a subcommittee for consideration. One of the first actions taken is the transmittal of copies of the bill to the departments or agencies concerned with the subject matter and frequently to the General Accounting Office with a request for an official report of views on the necessity or desirability of enacting the bill into law. Ample time is given for the submission of the reports and when received they are accorded serious consideration but are not binding on the committee in determining whether or not to act favorably on the bill. The reports of the executive departments and agencies are submitted first to the Office of Management and Budget to determine whether the bill is consistent with the program of the President.

COMMITTEE MEETINGS

Standing committees are required to have regular meeting days no less frequently than once a month, but the chairman may call and convene additional meetings. Three or more members of a standing committee may file with the committee a written request that the chairman call a special meeting. The request must specify the measure or matter to be considered. If the chairman fails, within three calendar days after the filing of the request, to call the requested special meeting, to be held within seven calendar days after the filing of the request, a majority of the members of the committee may call the special meeting by filing with the committee written notice specifying the time and date of the meeting and the measure or matter to be considered.

With the exception of the Committees on Appropriations, on the Budget, on Rules, and on Standards of Official Conduct, committees may not, without special permission, meet while the House is reading a measure for amendment under the "five-minute rule". (See first paragraph under heading "Second Reading" in Part XI.) In 1977, the House amended its rules to provide that special permission to meet will be given unless 10 or more Members object. Committees may meet during a recess up to the expiration of the constitutional term.

PUBLIC HEARINGS

If the bill is of sufficient importance, and particularly if it is controversial, the committee will usually set a date for public hearings. Each committee (except the Committee on Rules) is required to make public announcement of the date, place, and subject matter of any hearing to be conducted by the committee on any measure or matter at least one week before the commencement of that hearing, unless the committee determines that there is good cause to begin the hearing at an earlier date. If the committee makes that determination, it must make a public announcement to that effect at the earliest possible date. Public announcements are published in the Daily Digest portion of the Congressional Record as soon as possible after the announcement is made by the committee, and are often noted in newspapers and periodicals. Personal notice, usually in the form of a letter, but possibly in the form of a subpena, is frequently sent to individuals, organizations, and Government departments and agencies that are known to be interested.

Committee and subcommittee hearings are required to be public except when the committee or subcommittee, in open session and with a majority present, determines by roll call vote that all or part of the remainder of that hearing on that day shall be closed to the public because disclosure of testimony, evidence, or other matters to be considered would endanger the national security or would violate a law or Rule of the House of Representatives. The committee or subcommittee may by the same procedure vote to close one subsequent day of hearing.

Hearings on the budget are required to be held by the Committee on Appropriations in open session within 30 days after its transmittal to Congress, except when the committee, in open session and with a quorum present, determines by roll call vote that the testimony to be taken at that hearing on that day may be related to a matter of national security. The committee may by the same procedure close one subsequent day of hearing.

On the day set for the public hearing an official reporter is present to record the testimony in favor of and against the bill. Suitable accommodations are provided for the public and witnesses.

The bill may be read in full at the opening of the hearings and a copy is inserted in the record. After a brief introductory statement by the chairman and often by the ranking minority Member or other committee member, the first witness is called. Members or Senators who wish to be heard are given preference out of courtesy and because of the limitations on their time. Cabinet officers and high-ranking civil and military officials of the Government, as well as any private individual who is interested, may appear and testify either voluntarily or at the request or summons of the committee.

Committees require, so far as practicable, that witnesses who appear before it file with the committee, in advance of their appearance, a written statement of their proposed testimony and limit their oral presentations to a brief summary of their arguments.

Minority party members of the committee are entitled to call witnesses of their own to testify on a measure during at least one day of the hearing.

All committee rules in the House must provide that each Member shall have only five minutes in the interrogation of witnesses until each Member of the committee who desires to question a witness has had an opportunity to do so.

A typewritten transcript of the testimony taken at a public hearing is made available for inspection in the office of the clerk of the committee and frequently the complete transcript is printed and distributed widely by the committee.

BUSINESS MEETINGS

After hearings are completed the subcommittee usually will consider the bill in a session that is popularly known as the "mark-up" session. The views of both sides are studied in detail and at the conclusion of deliberation a vote is taken to determine the action of the subcommittee. It may decide to report the bill favorably to the full committee, with or without amendment, or unfavorably, or suggest that the committee "table" it, that is, postpone action indefinitely. Each member of the subcommittee, regardless of party affiliation, has one vote.

All meetings for the transaction of business, including the markup of legislation, of standing committees or subcommittees must be open to the public except when the committee or subcommittee, in open session with a majority present, determines by roll call vote that all or part of the remainder of the meeting on that day shall be closed to the public. However, the members of the committee may authorize congressional staff and departmental representatives to be present at any business or mark-up session that has been closed to the public. These provisions do not apply to open committee hearings, hearings on the budget, or to any meeting that relates solely to internal budget or personnel matters.

COMMITTEE ACTION

At committee meetings reports on bills may be made by subcommittees. Reports are fully discussed and amendments may be offered. Committee amendments are only proposals to change the bill as introduced and are subject to acceptance or rejection by the House itself. A vote of committee members is taken to determine the action of the full committee on the bill, that is usually either to report the bill favorably to the House, with or without amendments, or to table it. Because tabling a bill is normally effective in preventing action on it, adverse reports to the House by the full committee are not ordinarily made. On rare occasions, a committee may report a bill without recommendation or unfavorably.

Generally, a majority of the committee constitutes a quorum, the number of members who must be present in order for the committee to act. This ensures adequate participation by both sides in the action taken. However, the rules allow committees to vary the number of members necessary for a quorum for certain actions. For example, each committee may fix the number of its members, but not less than two, necessary for a quorum for taking testimony and receiving evidence. In 1977, the House amended its rules to allow committees (except the Committees on Appropriations, on the Budget, and on Ways and Means) to fix the number of its members, but not less than one-third, necessary for a quorum for taking certain other actions. The absence of a quorum is the subject of a point of order—that is, an objection that the proceedings are out of order—i.e., that the required number of members is not present.

PUBLIC INSPECTION OF RESULTS OF ROLL CALL VOTE IN COMMITTEE

The result of each roll call vote in any meeting of a committee must be made available by that committee for inspection by the public at reasonable times in the offices of that committee. Information available for public inspection includes a description of each amendment, motion, order, or other proposition; the name of each Member voting for and each Member voting against the amendment, motion, order, or proposition, and whether by proxy or in person; and the names of those Members present but not voting.

With respect to each roll call vote by a committee on a motion to report a bill or resolution of a public character, the total number of votes cast for, and the total number of votes cast against, the reporting of the bill or resolution must be included in the committee report.

PROXY VOTING

A vote by a Member of a committee with respect to a measure or other matter may not be cast by proxy unless that committee adopts a written rule that permits voting by proxy and requires that the proxy authorization (1) be in writing, (2) assert that the Member is absent on official business or is otherwise unable to be present at the meeting of the committee, (3) designate the person who is to execute the proxy authorization, and (4) be limited to a specific measure or matter and any amendments or motions pertaining to the measure or matter. A Member may authorize a general proxy only for motions to recess, adjourn or other procedural matters. A proxy must be signed by the Member and must contain the date and time of day that it is signed. A proxy may not be counted for a quorum.

POINTS OF ORDER WITH RESPECT TO COMMITTEE PROCEDURE

A point of order does not lie with respect to a measure reported by a committee on the ground that hearings on the measure were not conducted in accordance with required committee procedure; except that a point of order on that ground may be made by a Member of the committee which reported the measure if, in the committee, that point of order was (A) timely made and (B) improperly overruled or not properly considered.

BROADCASTING COMMITTEE HEARINGS AND MEETINGS

It is permissible to cover open committee hearings in the House by television, radio, and still photography. This permission is granted under well defined conditions outlined in clause 3(d) of Rule XI of the Rules of the House of Representatives. As stated in the rule:

The coverage of committee hearings and meetings by television broadcast, radio broadcast, or still photography is a privilege made available by the House and shall be permitted and conducted only in strict conformity with the purposes, provisions, and requirements of this clause.

VII. REPORTED BILLS

If the committee votes to report the bill favorably to the House one of the Members is designated to write the committee report. The report describes the purpose and scope of the bill and the reasons for its recommended approval. Generally, a section-by-section analysis is set forth in detail explaining precisely what each section is intended to accomplish. Under the rules of the House all changes in existing law must be indicated and the text of laws being repealed must be set out. This is known as the "Ramseyer" rule; a similar rule in the Senate is known as the "Cordon" rule. Committee amendments must also be set out at the beginning of the report and explanations of them are included. Executive communications requesting the introduction and consideration of the bill are usually quoted in full.

If at the time of approval of a bill by a committee (except the Committee on Rules) a Member of the committee gives notice of his intention to file supplemental, minority, or additional views, that Member is entitled to not less than three calendar days (Saturdays, Sundays and legal holidays excluded) in which to file those views with the clerk of the committee and they must be included in the report on the bill. Committee reports, with certain exceptions, must be filed while the House is actually sitting unless unanimous consent is obtained from the House to file at a later time.

The report is assigned a report number when it is filed, and it is delivered to the Government Printing Office for printing during that night. Beginning with the 91st Congress, in 1969, the report number contains a prefix-designator which indicates the number of the Congress. For example, the first House report in 1969 was numbered 91–1.

The bill also is printed when reported (see Fig. 2, p. 55) and committee amendments are indicated by showing new matter in italics and deleted matter in stricken-through type. The report number is also printed on the bill and the calendar number is shown on both the first and back pages of the bill. However, in the case of a bill that was referred to two or more committees for consideration in sequence, the calendar number is printed only on the bill as reported by the last committee to consider it. (See Part IX, "Calendars.")

Committee reports (see Fig. 3, p. 57) are perhaps the most valuable single element of the legislative history of a law. They are used by the courts, executive departments and agencies, and public generally, as a source of information regarding the purpose and meaning of the law.

CONTENTS OF REPORTS

The report of a committee on a measure that has been approved by the committee must include (A) the committee's oversight findings and recommendations, (B) the statement required by the Congressional Budget Act of 1974, if the measure provides new budget authority or new or increased expenditures, (C) the estimate and comparison prepared by the Director of the Congressional Budget Office whenever the Director has submitted that estimate and comparison to the committee prior to the filing of the report, and (D) a summary of the oversight findings and recommendations made by the Committee on Government Operations whenever they have been submitted to the legislative committee in a timely fashion to allow an opportunity to consider the findings and recommendations during the committee's deliberations on the measure. Each of these items are separately set out and clearly identified in the report.

INFLATIONARY IMPACT AND COST ESTIMATES IN REPORTS

Each report of a committee on a bill or joint resolution of a public character reported by the committee must contain a detailed analytical statement as to whether the enactment of the bill or joint resolution into law may have an inflationary impact on prices and costs in the operation of the national economy.

Each report also must contain an estimate, made by the committee, of the costs which would be incurred in carrying out that bill or joint resolution in the fiscal year reported and in each of the 5 fiscal years thereafter or for the duration of the program authorized if less than 5 years. In the case of a measure involving revenues, the report need contain only an estimate of the gain or loss in revenues for a 1-year period. The report must also include a comparison of the estimates of those costs with the estimate made by any Government agency and submitted to that committee. The Committees on Appropriations, on House Administration, on Rules, and on Standards of Official Conduct are not required to include cost estimates in their reports.

FILING OF REPORTS

Measures approved by a committee must be reported promptly after approval. A majority of the Members of the committee may file a written request with the clerk of the committee for the reporting of the measure. When the request is filed, the clerk immediately must notify the chairman of the committee of the filing of the request, and the report on the measure must be filed within seven days (exclusive of days on which the House is not in session) after the day on which the request is filed. This does not apply to the reporting of a regular appropriation bill by the Committee on Appropriations prior to compliance with requirements set out in the next paragraph, nor does it apply to a report of the Committee on Rules with respect to the rules, joint rules, or order of business of the House or to the reporting of a resolution of inquiry addressed to the head of an executive department.

Before reporting the first regular appropriation bill for each fiscal year, the Committee on Appropriations must, to the extent practicable and in accordance with the Congressional Budget Act of 1974, complete subcommittee markup and full committee action on all regular appropriation bills for that year and submit to the House a summary report comparing the Committee's recommendations with the appropriate levels of budget outlays and new budget authority as set forth in the most recently agreed to concurrent resolution on the budget for that year.

Generally, bills or resolutions that directly or indirectly authorize the enactment of new budget authority for a fiscal year must be reported to the House on or before May 15 preceding the beginning of that fiscal year. This deadline may be waived in emergency situations.

AVAILABILITY OF REPORTS AND HEARINGS

With certain exceptions (relating to emergency situations, such as a measure declaring war or other national emergency), a measure or matter reported by a committee (except the Committee on Rules in the case of a resolution making in order the consideration of a bill, resolution, or other order of business) may not be considered in the House until the third calendar day (excluding Saturdays, Sundays, and legal holidays) on which the report of that committee on that measure has been available to the Members of the House. In addition, the measure or matter may not be considered unless copies of the report and the reported measure or matter have been available to the Members for at least two hours before the beginning of consideration; however, it is always in order to consider a report from the Committee on Rules specifically providing for the consideration of a reported measure or matter notwithstanding this restriction. If hearings were held on a measure or matter so reported, the committee is required to make every reasonable effort to have those hearings printed and available for distribution to the Members of the House prior to the consideration of the measure in the House. General appropriation bills may not be considered until printed committee hearings and a committee report thereon have been available to the Members of the House for at least three calendar days (excluding Saturdays, Sundays, and legal holidays).

VIII. LEGISLATIVE REVIEW BY STANDING COMMITTEES

Under the Legislative Reorganization Act of 1970, each standing committee (other than the Committees on Appropriations, and on the Budget) is required to review and study, on a continuing basis, the application, administration, execution, and effectiveness of the laws dealing with the subject matter over which the committee has jurisdiction and the organization and operation of Federal agencies and entities having responsibility for the administration and evaluation of those laws. Prior to 1970, the Committees on Government Operations and on Appropriations had the oversight responsibility to review Government activities within their jurisdiction.

The purpose of the review and study is to determine whether laws and the programs created by Congress are being implemented and carried out in accordance with the intent of Congress and whether those programs should be continued, curtailed, or eliminated. In addition, each committee having oversight responsibility is required to review and study any conditions or circumstances that may indicate the necessity or desirability of enacting new or additional legislation within the jurisdiction of that committee, and must undertake, on a continuing basis, futures research and forecasting on matters within the jurisdiction of that committee. Each standing committee also has the function of reviewing and studying, on a continuing basis, the impact or probable impact of tax policies on subjects within its jurisdiction.

At the beginning of each Congress, a representative of the Committee on Government Operations meets with representatives of each of the other committees of the House to discuss the oversight plans of those committees and to assist in coordinating all of the oversight activities of the House during that Congress. Within 60 days after Congress convenes, the committee reports to the House the results of those meetings and discussions, and any recommendations which it has to assure the most effective coordination of oversight activities and otherwise achieve the oversight objectives.

In addition, several of the standing committees have special oversight responsibilities, the details of which are contained in the rules of the House.

IX. CALENDARS

A calendar of the House of Representatives, together with a history of all measures reported by a standing committee of either House, is printed each day the House is sitting for the information of those interested.

As soon as a bill is favorably reported, it is assigned a calendar number on either the Union Calendar or the House Calendar, the two principal calendars of business. The calendar number is printed on both the first and the back pages of the bill. In the case of a bill that was referred to two or more committees for consideration in sequence, the calendar number is printed only on the bill as reported by the last committee to consider it.

UNION CALENDAR

The rules of the House provide that there shall be:

First. A Calendar of the Committee of the Whole House on the state of the Union, to which shall be referred bills raising revenue, general appropriation bills, and bills of a public character directly or indirectly appropriating money or property.

This is commonly known as the Union Calendar and the large majority of public bills and resolutions are placed on it on being reported to the House.

HOUSE CALENDAR

The rules further provide that there shall be:

Second. A House Calendar, to which shall be referred all bills of a public character not raising revenue nor directly or indirectly appropriating money or property.

The public bills and resolutions that are not placed on the Union Calendar are referred to the House Calendar.

CONSENT CALENDAR

If a measure pending on either of these calendars is of a noncontroversial nature it may be placed on the Consent Calendar. The House rules provide that after a bill has been favorably reported and is on either the House or Union Calendar any Member may file with the Clerk a notice that he desires the bill placed upon the Consent Calendar. On the first and third Mondays of each month immediately after the reading of the Journal, the Speaker directs the Clerk to call the bills in numerical order (that is, in the order of their appearance on that calendar) that have been on the Consent Calendar for three legislative days. If objection is made to the consideration of any bill so called it is carried over on the calendar without prejudice to the next day when the Consent Calendar is again called, and if then objected to by three or more Members it is immediately stricken from the calendar and may not be placed on the Consent Calendar again during that Session of Congress. If objection is not made and if the bill is not "passed over" by request, it is passed by unanimous consent without debate. Ordinarily the only amendments considered are those sponsored by the committee that reported the bill.

To avoid the passage without debate of measures that may be controversial or are sufficiently important or complex to require full discussion there are six official objectors—three on the majority side and three on the minority side—who make a careful study of bills on the Consent Calendar. If a bill involves the expenditure of more than a fixed maximum amount of money or if it changes national policy or has other aspects that any of the objectors believes demand explanation and extended debate, it will be objected to and will not be passed by consent. That action does not necessarily mean the final defeat of the bill since it may then be brought up for consideration in the same way as any other bill on the House or Union Calendars.

PRIVATE CALENDAR

All bills of a private character, namely bills for relief in the nature of claims against the United States or private immigration bills, are referred to the Private Calendar which is called on the first and third Tuesdays of each month. If objection is made by two or more Members to the consideration of any measure called, it is recommitted to the committee that reported it. As in the case of the Consent Calendar there are six official objectors, three on the majority side and three on the minority side, who make a careful study of each bill or resolution on the Private Calendar and who will object to a measure that does not conform to the requirements for that calendar, thereby preventing the passage without debate of nonmeritorious bills and resolutions.

DISTRICT OF COLUMBIA BUSINESS

The second and fourth Mondays in each month, after the disposition of motions to discharge committees and after the disposal of business on the Speaker's table requiring only referral to committee, are set aside, when claimed by the Committee on the District of Columbia, for the consideration of any business that is presented by that committee.

X. OBTAINING CONSIDERATION OF MEASURES

Obviously certain measures pending on the House and Union Calendars are more important and urgent than others and it is necessary to have a system permitting their consideration ahead of those that do not require immediate action. Since all measures are placed on those calendars in the order in which they are reported to the House, the latest bill reported would be the last to be taken up if the calendar number alone were the determining factor.

SPECIAL RESOLUTIONS

To avoid delays and to provide some degree of selectivity in the consideration of measures, it is possible to have them taken up out of order by procuring from the Committee on Rules a special resolution or "rule" for their consideration. That committee, which is composed of majority and minority Members but with a larger proportion of majority Members than other committees, is specifically granted jurisdiction over resolutions relating to the order of business of the House. Usually the chairman of the committee that has favorably reported the bill appears before the Committee on Rules accompanied by the sponsor of the measure and one or more members of his committee in support of his request for a resolution providing for its immediate consideration. If the Rules Committee is satisfied that the measure should be taken up it will report a resolution reading substantially as follows with respect to a bill on the Union Calendar:

> *Resolved*, That immediately upon the adoption of this resolution it shall be in order for the House to resolve itself into the Committee of the Whole House on the State of the Union and proceed to consider the bill (H.R. ——) entitled, etc., debate to be limited to — hours, one-half to be controlled by the chairman of the Committee on ——, and one-half by the ranking minority member of such committee.

If the measure is on the House Calendar the resolution reads substantially as follows:

> *Resolved*, That immediately upon the adoption of this resolution the House shall proceed to consider the bill (H.R. ——) entitled, etc., and at the end of — hours a vote shall be taken on all pending amendments and on the bill to final passage.

The resolution may waive points of order against the bill. When it limits or prevents floor amendments, it is popularly known as a "closed rule".

CONSIDERATION OF MEASURES MADE IN ORDER BY PREVIOUS RESOLUTION

When a "rule" has been reported to the House, and is not considered immediately, it is referred to the calendar, and if not called up for consideration by the Member of the Rules Committee who made the report, within 7 legislative days thereafter any member of the Rules Committee may call it up as a question of privilege and the Speaker will recognize any Member of that Committee who seeks recognition for that purpose.

If, within 7 calendar days after a measure has, by resolution, been made in order for consideration by the House, a motion has not been offered for its consideration, the Speaker may, in his discretion, recognize a Member of the committee that reported the measure to offer a motion that the House consider it, if the Member has been duly authorized by that committee to offer the motion.

There are several other methods of obtaining consideration of bills that either have not been reported by a committee or, if reported, for which a special resolution or "rule" has not been obtained.

MOTION TO DISCHARGE COMMITTEE

A Member may present to the Clerk a motion in writing to discharge a committee from the consideration of a public bill or resolution that has been referred to it 30 days prior thereto. A Member may also file a motion to discharge the Committee on Rules from further consideration of a resolution providing either a special order of business, or a special rule for the consideration of a public bill or resolution favorably reported by a standing committee, or a special rule for the consideration of a public bill or resolution that has remained in a standing committee 30 days or more without action. This motion may be made only when the resolution, from which it is moved to discharge the Committee on Rules, has been referred to that committee at least seven days prior to the filing of the motion to discharge. The motion is placed in the custody of the Clerk, who arranges some convenient place for the signature of Members. When a majority of the total membership of the House have signed the motion it is entered on the Journal, printed with the signatures thereto in the Congressional Record, and referred to the Calendar of Motions to Discharge Committees.

On the second and fourth Mondays of each month, except during the last 6 days of a session, a Member who has signed a motion to discharge, that has been on the calendar at least 7 days, may seek recognition and be recognized for the purpose of calling up the motion. The bill or resolution is then read by title only. After 20 minutes' debate, one-half in favor of the proposition and one-half in opposition, the House proceeds to vote on the motion to discharge.

If the motion to discharge the Committee on Rules from a resolution pending before the committee prevails, the House immediately votes on the adoption of that resolution.

If the motion to discharge one of the standing committees of the House from a public bill or resolution pending before the committee prevails, a Member who signed the motion may move that the House proceed to the immediate consideration of the bill or resolution under the general rules of the House. If the House votes against the motion for immediate consideration, the bill or resolution is referred to its proper calendar with the same rights and privileges it would have had if reported favorably by the standing committee.

MOTION TO SUSPEND THE RULES

On Monday and Tuesday of each week and during the last 6 days of a session, the Speaker may entertain a motion to suspend the operation of the regular rules and pass a bill or resolution. Arrangement must be made in advance with the Speaker to recognize the Member who wishes to offer the motion. Before being considered by the House, the motion must be seconded by a majority of the Members present, by teller vote, if demanded. The motion to suspend the rules and pass the bill is then debated for 40 minutes, one-half by those in favor of the proposition and one-half by those opposed. The motion may not be amended and if amendments to the bill are proposed they must be included in the motion when it is made. The rules may be suspended and the bill passed only by affirmative vote of two-thirds of the Members voting, a quorum being present.

Except during the last 6 days of a session, the Speaker may postpone all recorded and yea-nay votes on motions to suspend the rules and pass bills and resolutions until the end of the day. At that time the House disposes of the deferred votes consecutively without further debate. By eliminating intermittent recorded votes on suspensions, this procedure reduces interruptions of committee meetings and also reduces the time Members spend on suspension days going back and forth between the floor and their committee rooms or offices.

If the Speaker intends to defer recorded and yea-nay votes on motions to suspend the rules and pass bills and resolutions, he must announce his intention before he entertains the first motion to suspend on any suspension day. The deferred votes are taken after debate is concluded on all suspension motions scheduled for that legislative day. After the first deferred vote is taken, the Speaker may reduce to not less than five minutes the time period for subsequent deferred votes. If the House adjourns before completing action on one or more deferred votes, these must be the first order of business on the next suspension day. On Private Calendar days, however, that calendar will be disposed of before the deferred suspension votes.

CALENDAR WEDNESDAY

On Wednesday of each week, unless dispensed with by unanimous consent or by affirmative vote of two-thirds of the Members voting, a quorum being present, the standing committees are called in alphabetical order. A committee when named may call up for consideration any bill reported by it on a previous day and pending on either the House or Union Calendar. Not more than two hours of general debate is permitted on any measure called up on Calendar Wednesday and all debate must be confined to the subject matter of the measure, the time being equally divided between those for and those against it. The affirmative vote of a simple majority of the Members present is sufficient to pass the measure.

PRIVILEGED MATTERS

Under the rules of the House certain matters are regarded as privileged matters and may interrupt the order of business, for example, reports from the Committee on Rules and reports from the Committee on Appropriations on the general appropriation bills.

At any time after the reading of the Journal, a Member, by direction of the appropriate committee, may move that the House resolve itself into the Committee of the Whole House on the State of the Union for the purpose of considering bills raising revenues, or general appropriation bills. General appropriation bills may not be considered in the House until three calendar days (excluding Saturdays, Sundays, and legal holidays) after printed committee reports and hearings on them have been available to the Members. The limit on general debate is generally fixed by unanimous consent.

Other examples of privileged matters are conference reports, certain amendments to measures by the Senate, and veto messages from the President of the United States. The Member in charge of such a matter may call it up at practically any time for immediate consideration. Usually, this is done after consultation with both the majority and minority floor leaders so that the Members of both parties will have advance notice and will not be taken by surprise.

XI. CONSIDERATION

Our democratic tradition demands that bills be given consideration by the entire membership with adequate opportunity for debate and the proposing of amendments.

COMMITTEE OF THE WHOLE HOUSE

In order to expedite the consideration of bills and resolutions the House resorts to a parliamentary usage that enables it to act with a quorum of only 100 Members instead of the normally requisite majority, that is, 218. This consists of resolving itself into the Committee of the Whole House on the State of the Union to consider a measure. All measures on the Union Calendar—involving a tax, making appropriations, or authorizing payments out of appropriations already made—must be first considered in the Committee of the Whole.

Debate on the resolution that the House resolve itself into the Committee of the Whole is limited to one hour unless the Members vote to extend the debate. If the resolution is adopted, the Speaker leaves his chair after appointing a Chairman to preside.

The special resolution or "rule" reported by the Committee on Rules to allow for immediate consideration of the measure fixes the length of the debate in the Committee of the Whole. This may vary according to the importance and controversial nature of the measure. As provided in the resolution the control of the time is divided equally—usually between the Chairman and the ranking minority Member of the committee that reported the measure. Members seeking to speak for or against the measure usually arrange in advance with the Member in control of the time on their respective side to be allowed a certain amount of time in the debate. Others may ask the Member speaking at the time to yield to them for a question or a brief statement. Frequently permission is granted a Member by unanimous consent to extend his remarks in the Congressional Record if sufficient time to make a lengthy oral statement is not available during actual debate.

The conduct of the debate is governed principally by the standing rules of the House that are adopted at the opening of each Congress. Another recognized authority is Jefferson's Manual that was prepared by Thomas Jefferson for his own guidance as President of the Senate from 1797 to 1801. The House, in 1837, adopted a rule that still stands, providing that the provisions of Jefferson's Manual should govern the House in all cases to which they are applicable and in which they are not inconsistent with the standing rules and orders of the House. In addition there is a most valuable compilation of precedents up to the year 1935 set out in Hinds' Precedents and Cannon's Precedents, consisting of 11 volumes, to guide the action of the House. Summaries of the House precedents prior to 1959 can be found in a single volume entitled Cannon's Procedure in the House of Representatives. A later volume, Deschler's Procedure in the House of Representatives, is a compilation of the parliamentary precedents of the House, in summary form, together with other useful related material, from 1959 through 1976. Recent rulings of the Speaker are set out as notes to the current House Manual. Most parliamentary questions arising during the course of debate are susceptible of ruling backed up by a precedent of action in a similar situation. The Parliamentarian of the House is present in the House Chamber in order to assist the Chairman or the Speaker in making a correct ruling on parliamentary questions.

SECOND READING

During the general debate an accurate account is kept of the time used on both sides and when all the time allowed under the rule has been consumed the Chairman terminates the debate. Then begins the "second reading of the bill", section by section, at which time amendments may be offered to a section when it is read. Under the House rules, a Member is permitted five minutes to explain his proposed amendment, after which the Member who is first recognized by the Chair is allowed to speak for five minutes in opposition to it; there is no further debate on that amendment, thereby effectively preventing any attempt at filibuster tactics. This is known as the "five-minute rule". There is, however, a device whereby a Member may offer a pro forma amendment—"to strike out the last word"— without intending any change in the language, and be allowed five minutes for debate, thus permitting a somewhat more comprehensive debate. Each amendment is put to the Committee of the Whole for adoption.

At any time after a debate is begun under the five-minute rule, on proposed amendments to a section or paragraph of a bill, the committee may by majority vote of the Members present, close debate on the section or paragraph. However, if debate is closed on a section or paragraph before there has been debate on any amendment that a Member has caused to be printed in the Congressional Record after the reporting of the bill by the committee but at least one day prior to floor consideration of the amendment, the Member who caused the amendment to be printed in the Record is given five minutes in which to explain the amendment, after which the first person to obtain the floor has five minutes to speak in opposition to it, and there is no further debate on that proposed amendment; but time for debate is not allowed when the offering of the amendment is dilatory. Material placed in the Congressional Record must indicate the full text of the proposed amendment, the name of the proponent Member, the number of the bill to which it will be offered and the point in the bill or amendment thereto where the amendment is intended to be offered, and must appear in a portion of the Record designated for that purpose.

When an amendment is offered, while the House is meeting in the Committee of the Whole, the Clerk is required to transmit to the majority committee table five copies of the amendment and five copies to the minority committee table, and at least one copy of the amendment to the majority cloak room and at least one copy to the minority cloak room.

THE COMMITTEE "RISES"

At the conclusion of the consideration of a bill for amendment, the Committee of the Whole "rises" and reports the bill to the House with the amendments that have been adopted. In rising the Committee of the Whole reverts back to the House and the Chairman of the Committee is replaced in the chair by the Speaker of the House. The House then acts on the bill and any amendments adopted by the Committee of the Whole.

ACTION BY THE HOUSE

Under the rules of the House debate is cut off by moving "the previous question". If this motion is carried by a majority of the Members voting, a quorum being present, all debate is cut off on the bill on which the previous question has been ordered. The Speaker then puts the question: "Shall the bill be engrossed and read a third time?" If this question is decided in the affirmative, the bill is read a third time by title only and voted on for passage. In 1965, the House rules were amended to abolish the third reading of the bill in full on demand of a Member—a practice that was sometimes used as a dilatory tactic.

If the previous question has been ordered by the terms of the special resolution or "rule" on a bill reported by the Committee of the Whole, the House immediately votes on whatever amendments have been reported by the Committee in the sequence in which they were reported. After completion of voting on the amendments, the House immediately votes on the passage of the bill with the amendments it has adopted.

In those cases where the previous question has not been ordered, the House may engage in debate lasting one hour, at the conclusion of which the previous question is ordered and the House votes on the passage of the bill. During the debate it is in order to offer amendments to the bill or to the Committee amendments.

Measures that do not have to be considered in the Committee of the Whole are considered in the House in the first instance in accordance with the terms of the special resolution limiting debate on the measure.

After passage of the bill by the House, a *pro forma* motion to reconsider it is automatically made and laid on the table—i.e., action is postponed indefinitely—to forestall this motion at a later date, because the vote of the House on a proposition is not final and conclusive on the House until there has been an opportunity to reconsider it.

MOTIONS TO RECOMMIT

After the previous question has been ordered on the passage of a bill or joint resolution, it is in order to make one motion to recommit the bill or joint resolution to a committee and the Speaker is required to give preference in recognition for that purpose to a Member who is opposed to the bill or joint resolution. This motion is normally not subject to debate. However, with respect to a motion to recommit with instructions after the previous question has been ordered, it is in order to debate the motion for ten minutes before the vote is taken, the time to be equally divided between the proponents and opponents of the motion.

QUORUM CALLS AND ROLL CALLS

In order to speed up and expedite quorum calls and roll calls, the rules of the House provide alternative methods for pursuing these procedures.

The rules provide that in the absence of a quorum, fifteen Members, including the Speaker, if there is one, are authorized to compel the attendance of absent Members. A call of the House is then ordered, and the Speaker is required to have the call taken by electronic device, unless in his discretion he names one or more clerks "to tell" the Members who are present. In that case the names of those present are recorded by the clerks, and entered in the Journal of the House and absent Members have not less than 15 minutes from the ordering of the call of the House to have their presence recorded. If sufficient excuse is not offered for their absence, by order of a majority of those present, they may be sent for by officers appointed by the Sergeant-at-Arms for that purpose, and their attendance secured and retained. The House then determines the conditions on which they may be discharged. Members who voluntarily appear are, unless the House otherwise directs, immediately admitted to the Hall of the House and they must report their names to the Clerk to be entered on the Journal as present. However, the former practice of presenting Members at the Bar of the House, during a call, is now obsolete, and Members now report to the Clerk and are recorded without being formally excused unless brought in under compulsion.

Whenever a quorum fails to vote on any question, and a quorum is not present and objection is made for that reason, unless the House adjourns, a call of the House is required to be taken by electronic device, unless the Speaker orders the call in the manner described above, and the Sergeant-at-Arms proceeds to bring in absent Members. The yeas and nays on the pending question are at the same time considered as ordered and an automatic roll call vote is taken. The Clerk calls the roll and each Member who is present may vote on the pending question as he answers to his name. After the roll call is completed, each Member, whose attendance was secured, is brought before the House by the Sergeant-at-Arms, where his presence is noted, he is given an opportunity to vote, and his vote is recorded. If those voting on the question and those who are present and decline to vote together make a majority of the House, the Speaker declares that a quorum is constituted, and the pending question is decided according to the will of the majority of those voting. Further proceedings under the call are considered as dispensed with. At any time after the roll call has been completed, the Speaker may entertain a motion to adjourn, if seconded by a majority of those present as ascertained by actual count by the Speaker; and if the House adjourns, all proceedings under this paragraph are vacated.

The rules prohibit points of no quorum (1) before or during the daily prayer, (2) during administration of the oath of office to the Speaker or any Member, (3) during the reception of messages from the President or the Senate, (4) in connection with motions incidental to a call of the House, and (5) against a vote in which the Committee of the Whole agrees to rise (but an appropriate point of no quorum would be permitted against a vote defeating a motion to rise). If the presence of a quorum has been established at least once on any day, further points of no quorum are prohibited (1) during the reading of the Journal, (2) between the time a Committee of the Whole rises and its Chairman reports, and (3) during the period on any legislative day when Members are addressing the House under special orders. The language prohibiting quorum calls "during any period" when Members are speaking under special orders includes the time between addresses delivered during this period as well as the addresses themselves. Furthermore, a quorum call is not in order when no business has intervened since the previous call. For the purposes of this provision, all the situations described above are not to be considered as "business."

In 1977, the House amended its rules to prohibit points of no quorum when a motion or proposition is pending in the House unless the Speaker has put the motion or proposition to a vote. However, the Speaker has the discretion to recognize a Member of his choice to move a call of the House.

The first time the Committee of the Whole finds itself without a quorum during any day the Chairman is required to order the roll to be called by electronic device, unless, in his discretion, he orders a call by naming clerks "to tell" the Members, as described above. After the call of the Committee, the Committee rises and the Chairman reports the names of the absentees to the House that are then entered on the Journal. If on a call a quorum appears, the Committee resumes its sitting without further order of the House. In 1974, the House amended its rules to provide for the expeditious conduct of quorum calls in the Committee of the Whole. The Chairman now may suspend a quorum call once he or she determines that a bare or minimum quorum has been reached, that is, 100 or more Members. Under such a short quorum call the Committee will not rise, and therefore Members' names will not be published. In 1977, the House again amended its rules on quorum calls to provide that once the presence of a quorum of the Committee of the Whole has been established for the day, quorum calls in the Committee are only in order when the Committee is operating under the five-minute rule and the Chairman has put the pending motion or proposition to a vote.

VOTING

There are four methods of voting in the Committee of the Whole, that are also employed, together with an additional method, in the House. These are the voice vote (viva voce), the division, the teller vote, the recorded vote, and the yea-and-nay vote that is used only in the House. If a Member objects to the vote on the ground that a quorum is not present, there may be an automatic roll call vote.

To obtain a voice vote the Chair states, "As many as are in favor (as the question may be) say 'Aye'." "As many as are opposed, say 'No'." The Chair determines the result on the basis of the volume of ayes and noes. This is the form in which the vote is ordinarily taken in the first instance.

If it is difficult to determine the result of a voice vote, a division may be demanded. The Chair then states that a division has been demanded and says "as many as are in favor will rise and stand until counted". After counting those in favor he calls on those opposed to stand and be counted, thereby determining the number in favor of and those opposed to the question.

If a demand for a teller vote is supported by one-fifth of a quorum (20 in the Committee of the Whole, and 44 in the House), the Chair appoints one or more tellers from each side and directs the Members in favor of the proposition to pass between the tellers and be counted. After counting, a teller announces the number in the affirmative, and the Chair then directs the Members opposed to pass between the tellers and be counted. When the count is stated by a teller, the Chair announces the result.

If any Member requests a recorded vote and that request is supported by at least one-fifth of a quorum, the vote is taken by electronic device, unless the Speaker, in his discretion, orders clerks "to tell", that is, record the names of those voting on each side of the question. After the recorded vote is concluded, the names of those voting together with those not voting are entered in the Journal. Members have not less than fifteen minutes to be counted from the time the recorded vote is ordered or the ordering of the clerks "to tell" the vote.

In addition to the foregoing methods of voting, in the House, if the yeas and nays are demanded, the Speaker directs those in favor of taking the vote by that method to stand and be counted. The assent of one-fifth of the Members present (as distinguished from one-fifth of a quorum in the case of a demand for tellers) is necessary for ordering the yeas and nays. When the yeas and nays are ordered (or a point of order is made that a quorum is not present) the Speaker directs that as many as are in favor of the proposition will, as their names are called, answer "Aye"; as many as are opposed will answer "No". The Clerk calls the roll and reports the result to the Speaker who announces it to the House. The Speaker is not required to vote unless his vote would be decisive.

ELECTRONIC VOTING

Under modern practice that went into effect on January 23, 1973, recorded and roll call votes are usually taken by electronic device, except when the Speaker, in his discretion, orders the vote to be recorded by other methods prescribed by the rules of the House, and in emergency situations, such as, the failure of the electronic device to function. In addition, quorum calls are generally taken by electronic device. Essentially the system works as follows: A number of vote stations are attached to selected chairs in the Chamber. Each station is equipped with a vote card slot and four indicators, marked "yea", "nay", "present", and "open". The "open" indicator is used only when a vote period is in progress and the system is ready to accept votes. Each Member is furnished with a personalized Vote–ID Card. A Member casts his vote by inserting his card into any one of the vote stations and depressing the appropriate push button indicator according to his choice. The machine records the votes and reports the result when the vote is completed. In the event the Member finds himself without his Vote–ID Card, he may still cast his vote by paper ballot, that he hands to the Tally Clerk, who may then record the vote electronically according to the indicated preference of the Member. The paper ballots are green for "yea", red for "nay", and amber for "present".

PAIRING OF MEMBERS

When a Member anticipates that he will be unavoidably absent at the time a vote is to be taken he may arrange in advance to be recorded as being either in favor of, or opposed to, the question by being "paired" with a Member who will also be absent and who holds contrary views on the question. A specific pair of this kind shows how he would have voted if he had been present. Occasionally, a Member who has arranged in advance to be paired, actually is present at the time of voting. He then votes as he would have voted if he had not been paired, and subsequently withdraws his vote and asks to be marked "present" to protect his colleague. This is known as a "live pair". If his absence is to continue for several days during which a number of different questions are to be voted upon he may arrange a "general pair". A general pair does not indicate how he would have voted on the question, but merely that he and the Member paired with him would not have been on the same side of the question.

Pairs are not counted in determining the vote on the question, but, rather, provide an opportunity for absent Members to express formally how they would have voted had they been present. Pairs are announced by the Clerk of the House and are listed in the Congressional Record immediately after the names of those Members not voting on the question.

SYSTEM OF LIGHTS AND BELLS

Because of the large number and the diversity of daily tasks that they have to perform it is not practicable for Members to be present in the House (or Senate) Chamber at every minute that the body is actually sitting. Furthermore, many of the routine matters do not require the personal attendance of all the Members. In order to procure their presence when needed for a vote or to constitute a quorum, systems of electric lights and bells or buzzers are provided in various parts of the Capitol Building and of the House and Senate Office Buildings.

In the House the Speaker has ordered that the bells and lights comprising the system be utilized as follows:

1 ring and 1 light on the left—Teller vote.

1 long ring followed by a pause and then 3 rings and 3 lights on the left—Start or continuation of a notice or short quorum call in the Committee of the Whole that will be vacated if and when 100 Members appear on the floor. Bells are repeated every five minutes unless the call is vacated or the call is converted into a regular quorum call.

1 long ring and extinguishing of 3 lights on the left—Short or notice quorum call vacated.

2 rings and 2 lights on the left—Recorded vote, yea-and-nay vote or automatic roll call vote by electronic device or by tellers with ballot cards. The bells are repeated five minutes after the first ring.

2 rings and 2 lights on the left followed by a pause and then 2 more rings—Automatic roll call vote or yea-and-nay vote taken by a call of the roll in the House. The bells are repeated when the clerk reaches the R's in the first call of the roll.

2 rings followed by a pause and then 6 rings—First vote under Suspension of the Rules when the Speaker has announced his intention to defer recorded votes until the end of the suspension business. 2 bells are repeated five minutes after the first ring. 6 bells are rung at the beginning of each subsequent postponed vote, on which the Speaker has reduced the vote time to the five-minute minimum.

3 rings and 3 lights on the left—Regular quorum call in either the House or in the Committee of the Whole by electronic device or by clerks. The bells are repeated five minutes after the first ring.

3 rings followed by a pause and then 3 more rings—Regular quorum call by a call of the roll. The bells are repeated when the Clerk reaches the R's in the first call of the roll.

4 rings and 4 lights on the left—Adjournment of the House.

5 rings and 5 lights on the left—Recess of the House.

12 rings at two second intervals with 6 lights on the left—Civil Defense Warning.

The red light indicates that the House is in session.

XII. ENGROSSMENT AND MESSAGE TO SENATE

The preparation of a copy of the bill in the form in which it has passed the House is sometimes a detailed and complicated process because of the large number and complexity of amendments to some bills adopted by the House. Frequently these amendments are offered during a spirited debate with little or no prior formal preparation. The amendment may be for the purpose of inserting new language, substituting different words for those set out in the bill, or deleting portions of the bill. It is not unusual to have more than 100 amendments, including those proposed by the committee at the time the bill is reported and those offered from the floor during the consideration of the bill in the chamber. Some of the amendments offered from the floor are written in longhand and others are typewritten. Each amendment must be inserted in precisely the proper place in the bill, with the spelling and punctuation exactly the same as it was adopted by the House. Obviously, it is extremely important that the Senate receive a copy of the bill in the precise form in which it has passed the House. The preparation of such a copy is the function of the enrolling clerk.

There is an enrolling clerk in each House, constituting a division of the office of the Clerk of the House of Representatives and of the Secretary of the Senate. He receives all the papers relating to the bill, including the official Clerk's copy of the bill as reported by the standing committee and each amendment adopted by the House. From this material he prepares the engrossed copy of the bill as passed, containing all the amendments agreed to by the House. (See Fig. 4, p. 58.) At this point the measure ceases technically to be called a bill and is termed "an act" signifying that it is the act of one body of the Congress, although it is still popularly referred to as a bill. The engrossed bill is printed on blue paper and a certificate that it passed the House of Representatives is signed by the Clerk of the House. The engrossed bill is delivered by a reading clerk to the Senate, while that body is actually sitting, in a rather formal ceremonious manner befitting the dignity of both Houses. The reading clerk is escorted into the chamber by the Secretary or another officer of the Senate and upon being recognized by the President of the Senate states that the House has passed the bill, giving its number and title, and requests the concurrence of the Senate.

XIII. SENATE ACTION

The President of the Senate refers the engrossed bill to the appropriate standing committee of the Senate in conformity with the rules. The bill is immediately reprinted and copies are made available in the document rooms of both Houses. (See Fig. 5, p. 59.) This printing is known as the "Act print" or the "Senate referred print".

COMMITTEE CONSIDERATION

Senate committees give the bill the same kind of detailed consideration as it received in the House, and may report it with or without amendment, or "table" it. A committee member who wishes to express his individual views, or a group of members who wish to file a minority report, may do so, if he or they give notice, at the time of the approval of the measure, of his or their intention to file supplemental, minority or additional views, in which event those views may be filed within three days with the clerk of the committee and they become a part of the report.

When a committee reports a bill, it is reprinted with the committee amendments indicated by line-through type and italics. The calendar number and report number are indicated on the first and back pages, together with the name of the Senator making the report. (See Fig. 6, p. 61.) The committee report and any minority or individual views accompanying the bill also are printed at the same time. (See Fig. 7, p. 63.) Any Senator may enter a motion to discharge a committee from further consideration of a bill that it has failed to report after what is deemed to be a reasonable time. If the motion is agreed to by a majority vote, the committee is discharged and the bill is placed on the Calendar of Business under the standing rules.

All committee meetings, including those to conduct hearings, must be open to the public. However, a majority of the members of a committee or subcommittee may, after discussion in closed session, vote in open session to close a meeting or series of meetings on the same subject for no longer than 14 days if it is determined that the matters to be discussed or testimony to be taken will disclose matters necessary to be kept secret in the interests of national defense or the confidential conduct of the foreign relations of the United States; relate solely to internal committee staff management or procedure; tend to reflect adversely on the reputation of an individual or may represent an unwarranted invasion of privacy of the individual; may disclose law enforcement information that is required to be kept secret; may disclose certain information regarding certain trade secrets; or may disclose matters required to be kept confidential under other provisions of law or Government regulation.

(35)

The rules of procedure in the Senate differ to a large extent from those in the House. At the time that a bill is reported (and in the Senate this is a more formal matter than in the House of Representatives because the Senator usually announces orally that he is submitting the report) the Senator who is making the report may ask unanimous consent for the immediate consideration of the bill. If the bill is of a noncontroversial nature and there is no objection the Senate may pass the bill with little or no debate and with only a brief explanation of its purpose and effect. Even in this instance the bill is subject to amendment by any Senator. A simple majority vote is necessary to carry an amendment as well as to pass the bill. If there is any objection the report must lie over one day and the bill is placed on the calendar.

Measures reported by standing committees of the Senate may not be considered unless the report of that committee has been available to Senate Members for at least three days (excluding Saturdays, Sundays, and legal holidays) prior to consideration of the measure in the Senate. This requirement, however, may be waived by agreement of the majority and minority leaders and does not apply in certain emergency situations.

There is only one Calendar of Business in the Senate, there being no differentiation, as there is in the House, between (1) bills raising revenue, general appropriation bills, and bills of a public character appropriating money or property, and (2) other bills of a public character not appropriating money or property.

At the conclusion of the morning business for each legislative day the Senate proceeds to the consideration of the Calendar of Business. Bills that are not objected to are taken up in their order, and each Senator is entitled to speak once and for five minutes only on any question. Objection may be interposed at any stage of the proceedings, but on motion the Senate may continue consideration after the call of the calendar is completed, and the limitations on debate then do not apply.

On any day but Monday, following the announcement of the close of morning business, any Senator obtaining recognition may move to take up any bill out of its regular order on the calendar. Usually, this is the majority leader. The five-minute limitation on debate does not apply to the consideration of a bill taken up in this manner, and debate may continue until the hour when the President of the Senate "lays down" the unfinished business of the day. At that point consideration of the bill is discontinued and the measure reverts back to the Calendar of Business and may again be called up at another time under the same conditions.

When a bill has been objected to and passed over on the call of the calendar it is not necessarily lost. The majority leader, after consulting the majority policy committee of the Senate and the minority leadership, determines the time at which it will be called up for debate. At that time, a motion is made to consider the bill. The motion, which is debatable, if made after the morning hour, is sometimes the occasion for lengthy speeches, on the part of Senators opposed to the measure, intended to prevent or defeat action. This is the tactic known as "filibustering". Upon obtaining the floor Senators may speak as long as they please but may not speak more than twice on any one question in debate on the same day without leave of the Senate. Debate, however, may be closed if 16 Senators sign a motion to that effect and the motion is carried by three-fifths of the total membership of the Senate.[1] Such a motion is voted on without debate on the second day after the day it is filed.

While a measure is being considered it is subject to amendment and each amendment, including those proposed by the committee that reported the bill, is considered separately. Generally there is no requirement that proposed amendments be germane to the subject matter of the bill except in the case of general appropriation bills. Under the rules of the Senate a "rider", that is, an amendment proposing substantive legislation to an appropriation bill is prohibited, but this prohibition may be suspended by two-thirds vote on a motion to permit consideration of such an amendment on one day's notice in writing. Debate on the measure must be germane during the first three hours after the morning hour unless determined to the contrary by unanimous consent or on motion without debate. After final action on the amendments the bill is ready for engrossment and the third reading, which is usually by title only, although if demanded, it must be read in full. The Presiding Officer then puts the question on the passage and the vote is usually taken viva voce although a yea-and-nay vote is in order if demanded by one-fifth of the Senators present. A simple majority is necessary for passage. Before an amended measure is cleared for its return to the House of Representatives (or an unamended measure is cleared for enrollment) a Senator who voted with the prevailing side, or who abstained from voting, may make a motion within the next two days to reconsider the action. If the measure was passed without a recorded vote, any Senator may make the motion to reconsider. That motion is usually tabled and its tabling constitutes a final determination. If, however, the motion is granted, the Senate, by majority vote, may either affirm its action, which then becomes final, or reverse it.

The original engrossed House bill, together with the engrossed Senate amendments, if any, is then returned to the House with a message stating the action taken by the Senate. Where amendments have been made by the Senate the message requests that the House concur in them.

---

[1] Until Jan. 12, 1959, the rules required the assent of two-thirds of the total membership of the Senate to close debate. From then until Mar. 7, 1975, the rules required the assent of two-thirds of the Senators present and voting.

XIV. FINAL ACTION ON AMENDED BILL

On their return to the House the official papers relating to the amended measure are placed on the Speaker's table to await House action on the Senate amendments. If the amendments are of a minor or noncontroversial nature the Chairman of the committee that originally reported the bill—or any Member—may, at the direction of the committee, ask unanimous consent to take the bill with the amendments from the Speaker's table and agree to the Senate amendments. At this point the Clerk reads the title of the bill and the Senate amendments. If there is no objection the amendments are then declared to be agreed to, and the bill is ready to be enrolled for presentation to the President. Lacking unanimous consent, bills that do not require consideration in the Committee of the Whole are privileged and may be called up from the Speaker's table by motion for immediate consideration of the amendments. A simple majority is necessary to carry the motion and thereby complete floor action on the measure. A Senate amendment to a House bill is subject to a point of order that it must first be considered in the Committee of the Whole, if, originating in the House, it would be subject to that point.

REQUEST FOR A CONFERENCE

If, however, the amendments are substantial or controversial the Member may request unanimous consent to take the bill with the Senate amendments from the Speaker's table, disagree to the amendments and request a conference with the Senate to resolve the disagreeing votes of the two Houses. If there is objection it becomes necessary to obtain a special resolution from the Committee on Rules unless the Speaker, in his discretion, recognizes a Member for a motion, authorized by the committee having jurisdiction over the subject matter of the bill, to disagree to the amendments and ask for a conference. If there is no objection to the request, or if the motion is carried, the Speaker then appoints the managers (as the conferees are called) on the part of the House and a message is sent to the Senate advising it of the House action. A majority of the Members appointed to be managers must have been supporters of the House position, as determined by the Speaker. The Speaker must name Members who are primarily responsible for the legislation and must include, to the fullest extent feasible, the principal proponents of the major provisions of the bill as it passed the House. The Speaker usually follows the suggestions of the Chairman of the committee in charge of the bill in designating the managers on the part of the House from among the Members of the committee. The number, as fixed by the Speaker, is frequently seven, consisting of five Members of the majority party and two of the minority, but may be greater on important bills. Representation of both major parties is an important attribute of all our parliamentary procedures but, in the case of conference committees, it is important that the views of the House on the House measure be fully represented.

If the Senate agrees to the request for a conference a similar committee is appointed by unanimous consent by the Presiding Officer of the Senate. Both political parties may be represented on the Senate conference committee also, but the Senate committee need not be the same size as the House committee.

The conference committee is sometimes popularly referred to as the "Third House of Congress".

The request for a conference can be made only by the body in possession of the official papers. Occasionally the Senate, anticipating that the House will not concur in its amendments, votes to insist on its amendments and requests a conference on passage of the bill prior to returning the bill to the House. This practice serves to expedite the matter because several days' time may be saved by the designation of the Senate conferees before returning the bill to the House. The matter of which body requests the conference is not without significance because the one asking for the conference acts last on the report to be submitted by the conferees.

AUTHORITY OF CONFEREES

Although the managers on the part of each House meet together as one committee they are in effect two separate committees, each of which votes separately and acts by a majority vote. For this reason the number of the respective managers is largely immaterial.

The conferees are strictly limited in their consideration to matters in disagreement between the two Houses. Consequently they may not strike out or amend any portion of the bill that was not amended by the Senate. Furthermore, they may not insert new matter that is not germane to the differences between the two Houses. Where the Senate amendment revises a figure or an amount contained in the bill, the conferees are limited to the difference between the two numbers and may not increase the greater nor decrease the smaller figure. Neither House may alone, by instructions, empower its managers to make a change in the text to which both Houses have agreed, but the managers for both bodies may be given that authority by a concurrent resolution adopted by a majority of each House.

When a disagreement to an amendment in the nature of a substitute is committed to a conference committee it is in order for the managers on the part of the House to propose a substitute which is a germane modification of the matter in disagreement, but the introduction of language in that substitute presenting a specific additional topic, question, issue, or proposition not committed to the conference committee by either House does not constitute a germane modification of the matter in disagreement. Moreover, their report may not include matter not committed to the conference committee by either House, nor may their report include a modification of any specific topic, question, issue, or proposition committed to the conference committee by either or both Houses if that modification is beyond the scope of that specific topic, question, issue, or proposition as committed to the conference committee.

An amendment by the Senate to a general appropriation bill which would be in violation of the rules of the House, if the amendment had originated in the House, or an amendment by the Senate providing for an appropriation on a bill other than a general appropriation bill, may not be agreed to by the managers on the part of the House, unless a specific authority to agree to such an amendment is first given by the House by a separate vote on each specific amendment.

MEETINGS AND ACTION OF CONFEREES

The meetings of the conferees are customarily held on the Senate side of the Capitol. In 1975, the House and the Senate adopted rules providing that conference meetings were to be open to the public except when the conferees of either the House or the Senate, in open session, determined by a roll call vote of a majority of those conferees present, that all or part of the remainder of the meeting on the day of the vote would be closed to the public. However, in 1977, the House amended its rules to require that conference meetings be open, unless the House, in open session, determines by a roll call vote of a majority of those Members voting that all or part of the meeting will be closed to the public. When the report of the conference committee is read in the House, a point of order may be made that the conferees did not comply with this requirement. If the point of order is sustained, the conference report is considered rejected by the House and a new conference is requested.

There are generally four forms of recommendations available to the conferees when reporting back to their bodies, *viz*, that:

    1. the Senate recede from all (or certain of) its amendments;

    2. the House recede from its disagreement to all (or certain of) the Senate amendments and agree thereto;

    3. the House recede from its disagreement to all (or certain of) the Senate amendments and agree thereto with amendments; and

    4. the House recede from all (or certain of) its amendments to the Senate amendments.

In many instances the result of the conference is a compromise growing out of the third type of recommendation available to the conferees. The complete report may, of course, be comprised of one, two, three, or all four of these recommendations with respect to the various amendments. Occasionally the conferees find themselves unable to reach an agreement with respect to one or more amendments and report back a statement of their inability to agree on those particular amendments. These may then be acted upon separately. This partial disagreement is, of course, not practicable where the Senate strikes out all after the enacting clause and substitutes its own bill which must be considered as a single amendment.

If they are unable to reach any agreement whatsoever the conferees report that fact to their respective bodies and the amendments are in the position they were before the conference was requested. New conferees may be appointed in either or both Houses. In addition, the Houses may instruct the conferees as to the position they are to take. The practice of instructing the original conferees at the time of their appointment is rarely used today.

After House conferees on any bill or resolution in conference between the two bodies have been appointed for twenty calendar days and have failed to make a report, the House rules provide for a motion of the highest privilege to instruct the House conferees or discharge them and appoint new conferees. Further, during the last 6 days of a session it is a privileged motion to move to discharge, appoint, or instruct House conferees after House conferees have been appointed 36 hours without having made a report.

CONFERENCE REPORTS

When the conferees, by majority vote of each group, have reached complete agreement (or find that they are able to agree with respect to some but not all amendments) they embody their recommendations in a report made in duplicate that must be signed by a majority of the conferees appointed by each body. The minority portion of the managers have no authority to file a statement of minority views in connection with the report. Starting with the 92d Congress, in 1971, the report is required to be printed in both Houses and must be accompanied by an explanatory statement prepared jointly by the conferees on the part of the House and the conferees on the part of the Senate. (See Fig. 8, p. 64.) The statement must be sufficiently detailed and explicit to inform the Congress as to the effect that the amendments or propositions contained in the report will have on the measure to which those amendments or propositions relate. The engrossed bill and amendments and one copy of the report are delivered to the body that is to act first on the report; namely, the body that had agreed to the conference requested by the other.

In the Senate the presentation of the report is always in order except when the Journal is being read or a point of order or motion to adjourn is pending, or while the Senate is dividing; and when received, the question of proceeding to the consideration of the report, if raised, is immediately voted on without debate. The report is not subject to amendment in either body and must be accepted or rejected as an entirety. If the time for debate on the adoption of the report is limited, the time allotted must be equally divided between the majority and minority party. If the Senate, acting first, does not agree to the report it may by majority vote order it recommitted to the conferees. When the Senate agrees to the report its managers are thereby discharged and it then delivers the original papers to the House of Representatives with a message advising that body of its action.

A report that contains any recommendations which go beyond the differences between the two Houses is subject to a point of order in its entirety. Any change in the text as agreed to by both Houses renders the report subject to the point of order and the matter is before the House *de novo*.

The presentation of the report in the House of Representatives is always in order, except when the Journal is being read, while the roll is being called, or the House is dividing on any proposition. The report is considered in the House and may not be sent to the Committee of the Whole on the suggestion that it contains matters ordinarily requiring consideration in that Committee. The report may not be received by the House if the required statement does not accompany it.

It is, however, not in order to consider either (1) a conference report or (2) an amendment (including an amendment in the nature of a substitute) proposed by the Senate to a measure reported in disagreement between the two Houses, by a conference report, that the conferees have been unable to agree, until the third calendar day (excluding any Saturday, Sunday, or legal holiday) after the report and accompanying statement have been filed in the House, and consideration then is in order only if the report and accompanying statement have been printed in the daily edition of the Congressional Record for the day on which the report and statement have been filed; but these provisions do not apply during the last 6 days of the session. Nor is it in order to consider a conference report or such amendment unless copies of the report and accompanying statement, together with the text of the amendment, have been available to Members for at least two hours before the beginning of consideration; however, it is always in order to call up for consideration a report from the Committee on Rules only making in order the consideration of a conference report or such amendment notwithstanding this restriction. The time allotted for debate on a conference report or such amendment is equally divided between the majority party and the minority party. If the House does not agree to a conference report that the Senate has already agreed to, the report may not be recommitted to conference because the Senate conferees are discharged when the Senate agrees to the report.

When a conference report is called up before the House containing matter which would be in violation of the rules of the House with respect to germaneness if the matter had been offered as an amendment in the House, and which is contained either (1) in a Senate amendment to that measure (including a Senate amendment in the nature of a substitute for the text of that measure as passed by the House) and accepted by the House conferees or agreed to by the conference committee with modification or (2) in a substitute agreed to by the conference committee, it is in order, at any time after the reading of the report is completed or dispensed with and before the reading of the statement, to make a point of order that nongermane matter, which must be specified in the point of order, is contained in the report. Under a 1974 amendment of the rules, it is also in order to make a point of order to nongermane Senate matter in the conference report that originally appeared in the Senate bill but was not included in the House-passed version. If the point of order is sustained, it is then in order for the Chair to entertain a motion, that is of high privilege, that the House reject the nongermane matter covered by the point of order. It is in order to debate the motion for forty minutes, one-half of the time to be given to debate in favor of, and one-half in opposition to, the motion. Notwithstanding the final disposition of a point of order made with respect to the report, or of a motion to reject nongermane matter, further points of order may be made with respect to the report, and further motions may be made to reject other nongermane matter in the conference report not covered by any previous point of order which has been sustained. If a motion to reject has been adopted, after final disposition of all points of order and motions to reject, the conference report is considered as rejected and the question then pending before the House is whether (1) to recede and concur with an amendment that consists of that portion of the conference report not rejected or (2) to insist on the House amendment with respect to nongermane Senate matter that originally appeared in the Senate bill but was not included in the House-passed version. If all motions to reject are defeated, then, after the allocation of time for debate on the conference report equally divided between the majority and minority parties, it is in order to move the previous question on the adoption of the conference report.

Similar procedures are available in the House when the Senate proposes an amendment to a measure that would be in violation of the rule against nongermane amendments, and thereafter it is (1) reported in disagreement by a committee of conference or (2) before the House and the stage of disagreement is reached.

The amendments of the Senate in disagreement may be voted on separately and may be adopted by a majority vote after the adoption of the conference report itself as though no conference had been had with respect to those amendments. The Senate may recede from all amendments, or from certain of its amendments, insisting on the others with or without a request for a conference with respect to them. If the House does not accept the amendments insisted on by the Senate the entire conference process begins again with respect to them.

CUSTODY OF PAPERS

The custody of the original official papers is important in conference procedure because either body may act only when in possession of the papers. As indicated above the request for a conference may be made only by the body in possession. The papers are then transmitted to the body agreeing to the conference and by it to the managers of the House that asked. The latter in turn carry the papers with them to the conference and at its conclusion turn them over to the managers of the House that agreed to the conference. The latter deliver them to their own House, that acts first on the report and then delivers the papers to the other House for final action on the report.

Each group of conferees, at the conclusion of the conference, retains one copy of the report that has been made in duplicate, and signed by a majority of the managers of each body—the House copy signed first by the House managers and the Senate copy signed first by its managers.

Obviously a bill cannot become a law of the land until it has been approved in identical terms by both Houses of the Congress. When the bill has finally been approved by both Houses all the original papers are transmitted to the enrolling clerk of the body in which the bill originated.

XV. ENROLLMENT

When the bill has been agreed to in identical form by both bodies—either without amendment by the Senate, or by House concurrence in the Senate amendments, or by agreement in both bodies to the conference report—a copy of the bill is enrolled for presentation to the President.

The preparation of the enrolled bill is a painstaking and important task since it must reflect precisely the effect of all amendments, either by way of deletion, substitution, or addition, agreed to by both bodies. The enrolling clerk of the House (with respect to bills originating in the House) receives the original engrossed bill, the engrossed Senate amendments, the signed conference report, the several messages from the Senate, and a notation of the final action by the House, for the purpose of preparing the enrolled copy. From these he must prepare meticulously the final form of the bill, as it was agreed to by both Houses, for presentation to the President. (See Fig. 9, p. 66.) On occasion there have been upward of 500 amendments, particularly after a conference, each of which must be set out in the enrollment exactly as agreed to, and all punctuation must be in accord with the action taken.

The enrolled bill is printed on parchment paper, with a certificate on the reverse side of the last page, to be signed by the Clerk of the House stating that the bill originated in the House of Representatives (or by the Secretary of the Senate when the bill has originated in that body). It is examined for accuracy by the Committee on House Administration (or by the Secretary of the Senate when the bill originated in that body). When the Committee is satisfied with the accuracy of the bill the Chairman of the Committee attaches a slip stating that it finds the bill truly enrolled and sends it to the Speaker of the House for his signature. All bills, regardless of the body in which they originated, are signed first by the Speaker and then by the President of the Senate. The Speaker and the President of the Senate may sign bills only while their respective House is actually sitting unless advance permission is granted to them to sign during a recess or after adjournment. After both signatures are affixed the bill is returned to the Committee for the purpose of being presented to the President for his action under the Constitution.

XVI. PRESIDENTIAL ACTION

The Constitution provides that—

Every Bill which shall have passed the House of Representatives and the Senate, shall, before it becomes a Law, be presented to the President of the United States.

In actual practice a clerk of the Committee on House Administration (or the Secretary of the Senate when the bill originated in that body) delivers the original enrolled bill to an employee at the White House and obtains a receipt, and the fact of the delivery is then reported to the House by the Chairman of the Committee. Delivery to a White House employee has customarily been regarded as presentation to the President and as commencing the 10-day Constitutional period for Presidential action.

Copies of the enrolled bill are usually transmitted by the White House to the various departments interested in the subject matter so that they may advise the President who, of course, cannot be personally familiar with every item in every bill.

If the President approves the bill he signs it and usually writes the word "approved" and the date, the only Constitutional requirement being that he sign it. (See Fig. 9, p. 66.)

The Supreme Court has stated that undoubtedly the President when approving bills may be said to participate in the enactment of laws, which the Constitution requires him to execute.

The bill may become law without the President's signature by virtue of the Constitutional provision that if he does not return a bill with his objections within 10 days (Sundays excepted) after it has been presented to him, it shall be a law in like manner as if he had signed it. (See Fig. 11, p. 68.) However, if the Congress by their adjournment prevent its return, it does not become law. The latter event is what is known as a "pocket veto", that is, the bill does not become law even though the President has not sent his objections to the Congress.

Notice of the signing of a bill by the President is usually sent by message to the House in which it originated and that House informs the other, although this action is not necessary to the validity of the act. The action is also noted in the Congressional Record.

A bill becomes law on the date of approval (or passage over the President's veto), unless it expressly provides a different effective date.

VETO MESSAGE

By the terms of the Constitution, if the President does not approve the bill "he shall return it, with his objections to that House in which it shall have originated, who shall enter the objections at large on their Journal, and proceed to reconsider it". It is the usual but not invariable rule that a bill returned with the President's objections, must be voted on at once and when laid before the House the question

(45)

on the passage is considered as pending. A vetoed bill is always privileged, and a motion to take it from the table is in order at any time.

The Member in·charge moves the previous question which is put by the Speaker, as follows: "The question is, Will the House on reconsideration agree to pass the bill, the objections of the President to the contrary notwithstanding?" The Clerk calls the roll and those in favor of passing the bill answer "Aye", and those opposed "No". If fewer than two-thirds of the Members present (constituting a quorum) vote in the affirmative the bill is killed, and a message is usually sent to the Senate advising that body of the decision that the bill shall not pass. If, however, two-thirds vote in the affirmative, the bill is sent with the President's objections to the Senate together with a message advising it of the action in the House.

There is a similar procedure in the Senate where again a two-thirds affirmative vote is necessary to pass the bill over the President's objections. If then passed by the Senate the measure becomes the law of the land notwithstanding the objections of the President, and it is ready for publication as a binding statute. (See Fig. 12, p. 69.)

XVII. PUBLICATION

One of the important steps in the enactment of a valid law is the requirement that it shall be made known to the people who are to be bound by it. Obviously, there would be no justice if the state were to hold its people responsible for their conduct before it made known to them the unlawfulness of such behavior. That idea is implicit in the Constitutional prohibition against enacting *ex post facto* laws. In practice, our laws are published immediately upon their enactment so that they may be known to the people.

If the President approves a bill, or allows it to become law without his signature, the original enrolled bill is sent from the White House to the Administrator of General Services for publication. If a bill is passed by both Houses over the objections of the President the body that last overrides the veto likewise transmits it. There it is assigned a public law number, and paginated for the Statutes at Large volume covering that session of the Congress. The public law numbers run in sequence starting anew at the beginning of each Congress, and since 1957 are prefixed for ready identification by the number of the Congress—e.g., the first public law of the 95th Congress is designated Public Law 95–1 and subsequent laws of this Congress will also contain the same prefix designator.

"SLIP LAWS"

The first official publication of the statute is in the form generally known as the "slip law". (See Fig. 10, p. 67.) In this form, each law is published separately as an unbound pamphlet. Since the beginning of the 82d Congress, in 1951, the slip laws have been printed by photoelectric offset process from the original enrolled bill. This process ensures accuracy and saves both time and expense in preparing the copy. A heading indicates the public law number and bill number, and the date of approval. If the statute has been passed over the veto of the President, or has become law without his signature because he did not return it with his objections, an appropriate statement is inserted in lieu of the usual notation of approval. (See Figs. 11 and 12, pp. 68 and 69.)

The Office of the Federal Register, General Services Administration, which prepares the slip laws, provides marginal editorial notes giving the citations to laws mentioned in the text and other explanatory details. Beginning in 1974, the marginal notes also give the United States Code classifications, thus enabling the reader immediately to determine where the statute will appear in the Code. Each slip law also includes an informative guide to the legislative history of the law consisting of the committee report number, the name of the committee in each House, as well as the date of consideration and passage in each House, with a reference to the Congressional Record by volume, year, and date. Since 1971, a reference to Presidential statements—relating to the approval of a bill (or the veto of a bill when the veto was overridden and the bill becomes law)—has been included in the legislative history in the form of a citation to the Weekly Compilation of Presidential Documents (for slip laws) and to the Public Papers of the Presidents (for the Statutes at Large volumes).

Copies of the slip laws are delivered to the document rooms of both Houses where they become available to officials and the public immediately. They may also be obtained by annual subscription or individual purchase from the Superintendent of Documents at the Government Printing Office.

A 1966 amendment of section 113 of title 1 of the United States Code, makes the "Slip Laws" issued under the authority of the Administrator of General Services, and the Treaties and Other International Act Series issued under the authority of the Secretary of State, competent evidence in all the courts, tribunals and public offices of the United States, and of the several States.

STATUTES AT LARGE

For the purpose of providing a permanent collection of the laws of each session of the Congress the bound volumes, which are called the United States Statutes at Large, are prepared by the General Services Administration. When the latest volume containing the laws of the first session of the 95th Congress becomes available it will be No. 91 in the series. Each volume contains a complete index and a table of contents and, since 1956, a table of earlier laws affected, as well as a most useful table showing the legislative history of each law in the volume. There are also extensive marginal notes referring to laws in earlier volumes and earlier and later matters in the same volume.

Under the provisions of a statute originally enacted in 1895 these volumes are legal evidence of the laws contained in them and will be accepted as proof of those laws in any court in the United States.

The Statutes at Large are only a chronological arrangement of the laws exactly as they have been enacted. There is no attempt to arrange the laws according to their subject matter or to show the present status of an earlier law that has been amended on one or more occasions. That is the function of a code of laws.

UNITED STATES CODE

The United States Code contains a consolidation and codification of the general and permanent laws of the United States arranged according to subject matter under fifty title headings, in alphabetical order to a large degree. It sets out the current status of the laws, as amended, without repeating all the language of the amendatory acts except where necessary for that purpose and is declared to be prima facie evidence of those laws. Its purpose is to present the laws in a concise and usable form without requiring recourse to the many volumes of the Statutes at Large containing the individual amendments.

The Code is prepared by the Law Revision Counsel of the House of Representatives. New editions are published every six years and cumulative supplements are published after the conclusion of each regular session of the Congress.

Nineteen of the fifty titles have been revised and enacted as law, and one has been eliminated by consolidation with another. Those titles are now legal evidence of the law and the courts will receive them as proof of those laws. It is hoped that eventually all the titles will be revised and enacted into law and that thereafter they will be kept up to date by direct amendment.

APPENDIX

SELECT LIST OF GOVERNMENT PUBLICATIONS

*Constitution of the United States of America, Analysis and Interpretation, with annotations of cases decided by the Supreme Court of the United States to June 29, 1972; prepared by the Congressional Research Service, Library of Congress, Johnny H. Killian, editor, and Lester S. Jayson, supervising editor. Supplements published periodically.

*House Rules and Manual:
    Constitution, Jefferson's Manual and Rules of the House of Representatives of the United States, prepared by Wm. Holmes Brown, Parliamentarian. New editions are published each Congress.

*Senate Manual:
    Containing the standing rules, orders, laws, and resolutions affecting the business of the United States Senate; Jefferson's Manual, Declaration of Independence, Articles of Confederation, Constitution of the United States, etc. Prepared under the direction of the Senate Committee on Rules and Administration. New editions are published each Congress.

*Hinds' Precedents of the House of Representatives:
    Including references to provisions of the Constitution, laws, and decisions of the Senate, by Asher C. Hinds.
        Vols. 1–5 (1907).
        Vols. 6–8 (1935), as compiled by Clarence Cannon, are supplementary to vols. 1–5 and cover the 28-year period from 1907 to 1935, revised up to and including the 73d Congress.
        Vols. 9–11 (1941) are index-digest to vols. 1–5. [Now in the process of revision.]

*Cannon's Procedure in the House of Representatives:
    By Clarence Cannon, A.M., LL.B., LL.D., Member of Congress, sometime Parliamentarian of the House, Speaker pro tempore, Chairman of the Committee of the Whole, Chairman of Committee on Appropriations, etc.

*Deschler's Procedure in the U.S. House of Representatives:
    By Lewis Deschler, M.P.L., J.D., L.L.D., Parliamentarian of the House (1928–1974).

*Senate Procedure:
    By Floyd M. Riddick, Parliamentarian of the Senate: Senate Document No. 93–21 (1974).

Calendars of the House of Representatives and History of Legislation:
    Published each day the House is in session; prepared under the direction of the Clerk of the House of Representatives.

Committee Calendars:
    Published periodically by most of the standing committees of the House of Representatives and Senate, containing the history of bills and resolutions referred to the particular committee.

*Digest of Public General Bills and Resolutions:
    A brief synopsis of public bills and resolutions, and changes made therein during the legislative process; prepared by American Law Division, Congressional Research Service, Library of Congress, and published during each session in 5 or more cumulative issues with biweekly supplementation as needed.

*Congressional Record:
    Proceedings and debates of the House and Senate, published daily, and bound with an index and history of bills and resolutions at the conclusion of each session of the Congress.†

---

*For sale by the Superintendent of Documents, Government Printing Office, Washington, D.C. 20402.

†The record of debates prior to 1874 was published in the Annals of Congress (1789–1824), The Register of Debates (1824–1837), and the Congressional Globe (1833–1873).

Journal of the House cf Representatives:
Official record of the proceedings of the House, published at the conclusion of each session under the direction of the Clerk of the House.

Journal of the United States Senate:
Official record of the proceedings of the Senate, published at the conclusion of each session under the direction of the Secretary of the Senate.

*United States Statutes at Large:
Containing the laws and concurrent resolutions enacted, and reorganization plans and proclamations promulgated during each session of the Congress, published annually under the direction of the Administrator of General Services by the Office of the Federal Register, National Archives and Records Service, General Services Administration, Washington, D.C. 20408.
Supplemental volume: Tables of Laws Affected, Volumes 70–84 (1956–70), containing tables of prior laws amended, repealed, or patently affected by provisions of public laws enacted during that period.
Additional parts, containing treaties and international agreements other than treaties, published annually under the direction of the Secretary of State until 1950

*United States Treaties and Other International Agreements:
Compiled and published annually since 1950 under the direction of the Secretary of State.

*Treaties and Other International Agreements of the United States of America, 1776–1949:
A consolidation of the texts of treaties and other international agreements prior to 1950, compiled under the direction of Charles I. Bevans, Assistant Legal Adviser, Department of State, volumes I–XII (index volume in preparation).

*United States Code:
The general and permanent laws of the United States in force on the day preceding the commencement of the session following the last session the legislation of which is included; arranged in 50 titles; prepared under the direction and supervision of the Law Revision Counsel of the House of Representatives. New editions are published every 6 years and cumulative supplements are published annually.

*Federal Register:
Presidential Proclamations, Executive Orders, and Federal agency orders, regulations, and notices, and general documents of public applicability and legal effect, published daily. The regulations therein amend the Code of Federal Regulations. Published by the Office of the Federal Register, National Archives and Records Service, General Services Administration, Washington, D.C. 20408.

*Code of Federal Regulations:
Cumulates in bound volumes the general and permanent rules and regulations of Federal agencies published in the Federal Register, including Presidential documents. Each volume of the Code is revised at least once each calendar year and issued on a quarterly basis approximately as follows: Titles 1–16 as of January 1; Titles 17–27 as of April 1; Titles 28–41 as of July 1; and Titles 42–50 as of October 1. Published by the Office of the Federal Register, National Archives and Records Service, General Services Administration, Washington, D.C. 20408.

*Weekly Compilation of Presidential Documents:
Containing statements, messages, and other Presidential materials released by the White House up to 5:00 p.m. Friday of each week, published every Monday by the Office of the Federal Register, National Archives and Records Service, General Services Administration, Washington, D.C. 20408.

*Public papers of the Presidents of the United States:
Containing public messages and statements, verbatim transcript of the President's News Conference and other selected papers released by the White House each year, since 1945, compiled by the Office of the Federal Register, National Archives and Records Service, General Services Administration, Washington, D.C. 20408.

*Enactment of a Law, by Murray Zweben, Parliamentarian of the Senate, under the direction of Francis R. Valeo, Secretary of the Senate: Senate Document No. 152, 94th Congress, 2d Session, 1976.

History of the United States House of Representatives, by Dr. George B. Galloway, Senior Specialist in American Government, Legislative Reference Service, Library of Congress: House Document No. 250, 89th Congress, 1st Session, 1965. [New edition in preparation.]

Veto Power of the President, by Charles J. Zinn: Committee Print of the House Committee on the Judiciary, 82d Congress, 1st Session, 1951.

Extent of the Control of the Executive by the Congress of the United States, by Dr. Charles J. Zinn: Committee Print of the House Committee on Government Operations, 87th Congress, 2d Session, 1962.

*Our American Government, What Is It? How Does It Function? House Document No. 257, 95th Congress, 1st Session, 1978.

[Figure 1—Introduced Print*]

90TH CONGRESS
1ST SESSION

H. R. 8629

IN THE HOUSE OF REPRESENTATIVES

APRIL 17, 1967

Mr. CELLER introduced the following bill; which was referred to the Committee on the Judiciary

A BILL

To amend the Act of July 4, 1966 (Public Law 89–491).

1   *Be it enacted by the Senate and House of Representa-*

2   *tives of the United States of America in Congress assembled,*

3   That the Act of July 4, 1966 (80 Stat. 259), is hereby

4   amended as follows:

5   1. By adding in section 2 (b) (3) the words "the

6   Secretary of Commerce," after the words, "the Secretary

7   of Defense,".

8   2. By deleting in section 3 (d) the words "two years

9   after the date of the enactment of this Act," and inserting

10   in lieu thereof "July 4, 1969.".

*All illustrations in this document are reduced in size.

1   3. By deleting section 7 (a) and inserting in lieu thereof

2 the following:

3   "SEC. 7. (a) There are authorized to be appropriated

4 without fiscal year limitation such sums as may be necessary

5 for the expenses of the Commission."

[Figure 2—Reported Print]

Union Calendar No. 182

90TH CONGRESS
1ST SESSION

H. R. 8629

[Report No. 509]

IN THE HOUSE OF REPRESENTATIVES

APRIL 17, 1967

Mr. CELLER introduced the following bill; which was referred to the Committee on the Judiciary

JULY 25, 1967

Reported with an amendment, committed to the Committee of the Whole House on the State of the Union, and ordered to be printed

[Omit the part struck through and insert the part printed in italic]

A BILL

To amend the Act of July 4, 1966 (Public Law 89-491).

1   *Be it enacted by the Senate and House of Representa-*

2   *tives of the United States of America in Congress assembled,*

3   That the Act of July 4, 1966 (80 Stat. 259), is hereby

4   amended as follows:

5   1. By adding in section 2 (b) (3) the words "the

6   Secretary of Commerce," after the words, "the Secretary

7   of Defense,".

8   2. By deleting in section 3 (d) the words "two years

9   after the date of the enactment of this Act," and inserting

10   in lieu thereof "July 4, 1969.".

1   3. By deleting section 7 (a) and inserting in lieu thereof

2 the following:

3   ~~"SEC. 7. (a) There are authorized to be appropriated~~

4 ~~without fiscal year limitation such sums as may be necessary~~

5 ~~for the expenses of the Commission."~~

6   *"SEC. 7. (a) There is authorized to be appropriated not*

7 *to exceed $450,000 for the period through fiscal year 1969."*

[Figure 3—House Committee Report*]

90TH CONGRESS } HOUSE OF REPRESENTATIVES { REPORT
1st Session } { No. 509

AMERICAN REVOLUTION BICENTENNIAL COMMISSION

JULY 25, 1967.—Committed to the Committee of the Whole House on the State of the Union and ordered to be printed

Mr. ROGERS of Colorado, from the Committee on the Judiciary, submitted the following

REPORT

[To accompany H.R. 8629]

The Committee on the Judiciary, to whom was referred the bill (H.R. 8629) to amend the act of July 4, 1966 (Public Law 89-491), having considered the same, report favorably thereon with an amendment and recommend that the bill do pass.

The amendment is as follows:

On page 2, strike lines 3 through 5 and insert in lieu thereof the following:

"SEC. 7. (a) There is authorized to be appropriated not to exceed $450,000 for the period through fiscal year 1969."

EXPLANATION OF AMENDMENT

The purpose of the amendment is to limit the authorization for appropriations to $450,000 during the period through fiscal year 1969.

PURPOSE OF THE BILL

The purpose of H.R. 8629 is threefold: First, it would add the Secretary of Commerce as an ex officio member of the Commission; second, it would extend the date on which the Commission shall report to the President by 1 year—from July 4, 1968, to July 4, 1969; third, it would authorize the appropriation of public funds to finance the work of the Commission.

STATEMENT

Public Law 89-491, approved July 4, 1966, established the American Revolution Bicentennial Commission to commemorate the American

[Rule XIII of the Rules of the House now require the report to contain an estimate of the costs involved in the reported bill except as to certain committees. Rule XI also requires that when a record vote is taken, on a bill being reported by a committee, the report shall include the result of that vote]

*First page only.

[Figure 4—Engrossed Bill*]

90TH CONGRESS
1ST SESSION

H. R. 8629

AN ACT

To amend the Act of July 4, 1966 (Public Law 89–491).

1   *Be it enacted by the Senate and House of Representa-*

2 *tives of the United States of America in Congress assembled,*

3 That the Act of July 4, 1966 (80 Stat. 259), is hereby

4 amended as follows:

5   1. By adding in section 2 (b) (3) the words "the

6 Secretary of Commerce," after the words, "the Secretary

7 of Defense,".

8   2. By deleting in section 3 (d) the words "two years

9 after the date of the enactment of this Act," and inserting

10 in lieu thereof "July 4, 1969.".

11   3. By deleting section 7 (a) and inserting in lieu thereof

12 the following:

13   "SEC. 7. (a) There is authorized to be appropriated not

14 to exceed $450,000 for the period through fiscal year 1969."

Passed the House of Representatives August 7, 1967.

Attest: W. PAT JENNINGS,

Clerk.

*Printed on blue paper.

[Figure 5—Senate Referred ("Act") Print]

90TH CONGRESS
1ST SESSION

H. R. 8629

IN THE SENATE OF THE UNITED STATES

AUGUST 8, 1967

Read twice and referred to the Committee on the Judiciary

AN ACT

To amend the Act of July 4, 1966 (Public Law 89–491).

1   *Be it enacted by the Senate and House of Representa-*

2   *tives of the United States of America in Congress assembled,*

3   That the Act of July 4, 1966 (80 Stat. 259), is hereby

4   amended as follows:

5   1. By adding in section 2 (b) (3) the words "the Sec-

6   retary of Commerce," after the words, "the Secretary of

7   Defense,".

8   2. By deleting in section 3 (d) the words "two years

9   after the date of the enactment of this Act," and inserting

10   in lieu thereof "July 4, 1969.".

1   3. By deleting section 7 (a) and inserting in lieu thereof

2 the following:

3   "SEC. 7. (a) There is authorized to be appropriated not

4 to exceed $450,000 for the period through fiscal year 1969."

Passed the House of Representatives August 7, 1967.

Attest: W. PAT JENNINGS,

Clerk.

[Figure 6—Senate Reported Print]

Calendar No. 592

90TH CONGRESS
1ST SESSION

H. R. 8629

[Report No. 609]

IN THE SENATE OF THE UNITED STATES

AUGUST 8, 1967

Read twice and referred to the Committee on the Judiciary

OCTOBER 11 (legislative day, OCTOBER 10), 1967
Reported by Mr. DIRKSEN, with an amendment

[Insert the part printed in italic]

AN ACT

To amend the Act of July 4, 1966 (Public Law 89–491).

1 　　*Be it enacted by the Senate and House of Representa-*

2 *tives of the United States of America in Congress assembled,*

3 That the Act of July 4, 1966 (80 Stat. 259), is hereby

4 amended as follows:

5 　　1. By adding in section 2 (b) (3) the words "the

6 Secretary of Commerce," after the words, "the Secretary

7 of Defense,".

8 　　2. By deleting in section 3 (d) the words "two years

9 after the date of the enactment of this Act," and inserting

10 in lieu thereof "July 4, 1969.".

1   3. By deleting section 7 (a) and inserting in lieu thereof
2 the following:

3   "SEC. 7. (a) There is authorized to be appropriated not
4 to exceed $450,000 for the period through fiscal year 1969."

5   *4. By deleting in section 2(b)(1) the word "Four"*
6 *and inserting in lieu thereof the word "Six"; and by deleting*
7 *in section 2(b)(2) the word "Four" and inserting in lieu*
8 *thereof the word "Six".*

Passed the House of Representatives August 7, 1967.

Attest: W. PAT JENNINGS,
                                        Clerk.

Calendar No. 592

90TH CONGRESS *1st Session*	SENATE	REPORT No. 609

EXTENDING THE AMERICAN REVOLUTION BICENTENNIAL COMMISSION

OCTOBER 11 (legislative day, OCTOBER 10), 1967.—Ordered to be printed

Mr. DIRKSEN, from the Committee on the Judiciary, submitted the following

REPORT

[To accompany H.R. 8629]

The Committee on the Judiciary, to which was referred the bill (H.R. 8629) to amend the act of July 4, 1966 (Public Law 89–491), having considered the same, reports favorably thereon with an amendment and recommends that the bill as amended do pass.

AMENDMENT

On page 2, after line 4, insert the following:

4. By deleting in section 2(b)(1) the word "Four" and inserting in lieu thereof the word "Six"; and by deleting in section 2(b)(2) the word "Four" and inserting in lieu thereof the word "Six".

PURPOSE OF AMENDMENT

The purpose of the amendment is to increase the Senate membership on the Commission from four members to six members, and to increase the House of Representatives membership on the Commission from four members to six members.

PURPOSE

The purpose of the proposed legislation, as amended, is fourfold: First, it would add the Secretary of Commerce as an exofficio member of the Commission; second, it would extend the date on which the

[With certain exceptions, the Legislative Reorganization Act of 1970, requires the report to contain an estimate of the costs involved in the bill]

---

*First page only.

[Figure 8—Conference Committee Report]

90TH CONGRESS *1st Session*	HOUSE OF REPRESENTATIVES	REPORT No. 987

AMERICAN REVOLUTION BICENTENNIAL COMMISSION

NOVEMBER 28, 1967.—Ordered to be printed

Mr. ROGERS of Colorado, from the committee of conference, submitted the following

CONFERENCE REPORT

[To accompany H.R. 8629]

The committee of conference on the disagreeing votes of the two Houses on the amendment of the Senate to the bill (H.R. 8629) to amend the act of July 4, 1966 (Public Law 89–491), having met, after full and free conference, have agreed to recommend and do recommend to their respective Houses as follows:

That the Senate recede from its amendment.

BYRON G. ROGERS,
BASIL WHITENER,
ANDREW JACOBS, Jr.,
RICHARD H. POFF,
CHARLES E. WIGGINS,
Managers on the Part of the House.

EVERETT M. DIRKSEN,
JOHN L. McCLELLAN,
Managers on the Part of the Senate.

STATEMENT OF THE MANAGERS ON THE PART OF THE HOUSE

The managers on the part of the House at the conference on the disagreeing votes of the two Houses on the amendment of the Senate to the bill (H.R. 8629) to amend the act of July 4, 1966 (Public Law 89–491), submit the following statement in explanation of the effect of the action agreed upon by the conferees and recommended in the accompanying conference report:

The Senate passed H.R. 8629 with an amendment. The House disagreed to the amendment and requested a conference; the Senate then agreed to the conference.

H.R. 8629 as it passed the House added the Secretary of Commerce as an ex officio member of the American Revolution Bicentennial Commission, extended the time within which the Commission shall report to the President to July 4, 1969, and authorized the appropriation of funds to finance the work of the Commission.

These provisions are not in disagreement.

The Senate amendment added a provision which increased from four members to six members each the House and Senate membership on the Commission.

The conference report recommends that the Senate recede from its amendment.

BYRON G. ROGERS,
BASIL WHITENER,
ANDREW JACOBS, Jr.,
RICHARD H. POFF,
CHARLES E. WIGGINS,

Managers on the Part of the House.

[Legislative Reorganization Act of 1970, and the Rules of the House now require the statement to be prepared jointly by conferees on the part of the House and conferees on the part of the Senate]

FORMAT OF JOINT EXPLANATORY STATEMENT OF THE
COMMITTEE OF CONFERENCE

The managers on the part of the House and the Senate at the conference on the disagreeing votes of the two Houses on the amendment(s) of the House (Senate) to the bill (joint resolution) [number] ____ (title) ____ submit the following joint statement to the House and the Senate in explanation of the effect of the action agreed upon by the managers and recommended in the accompanying conference report.

—— ——,   —— ——,
—— ——,   —— ——,
—— ——,   —— ——,

Managers on the part   *Managers on the part*
of the House.   *of the Senate.*

[Figure 9—Enrolled Bill Signed by President]

H. R. 8629   PUBLIC LAW 90-187

Ninetieth Congress of the United States of America

AT THE FIRST SESSION

*Begun and held at the City of Washington on Tuesday, the tenth day of January,
one thousand nine hundred and sixty-seven*

An Act

To amend the Act of July 4, 1966 (Public Law 89-491).

*Be it enacted by the Senate and House of Representatives of the
United States of America in Congress assembled,* That the Act of
July 4, 1966 (80 Stat. 259), is hereby amended as follows:

1. By adding in section 2(b)(3) the words "the Secretary of Commerce," after the words, "the Secretary of Defense,"..

2. By deleting in section 3(d) the words "two years after the date
of the enactment of this Act," and inserting in lieu thereof "July 4,
1969.".

3. By deleting section 7(a) and inserting in lieu thereof the
following:

"SEC. 7. (a) There is authorized to be appropriated not to exceed
$450,000 for the period through fiscal year 1969."

Speaker of the House of Representatives.

*Vice President of the United States and
President of the Senate.*

APPROVED

DEC 12 1957

[Figure 10—Slip law]

Public Law 90-187
90th Congress, H. R. 8629
December 12, 1967

An Act

81 STAT. 567

To amend the Act of July 4, 1966 (Public Law 89-491).

Be it enacted by the Senate and House of Representatives of the United States of America in Congress assembled, That the Act of July 4, 1966 (80 Stat. 259), is hereby amended as follows:

1. By adding in section 2(b)(3) the words "the Secretary of Commerce," after the words, "the Secretary of Defense,".

2. By deleting in section 3(d) the words "two years after the date of the enactment of this Act," and inserting in lieu thereof "July 4, 1969.".

3. By deleting section 7(a) and inserting in lieu thereof the following:

"SEC. 7. (a) There is authorized to be appropriated not to exceed $450,000 for the period through fiscal year 1969."

Approved December 12, 1967.

American Revolution Bicentennial Commission.

Appropriation.

LEGISLATIVE HISTORY:

HOUSE REPORTS: No. 509 (Comm. on the Judiciary) and No. 987 (Comm. of
               Conference).
SENATE REPORT No. 609 (Comm. on the Judiciary).
CONGRESSIONAL RECORD, Vol. 113 (1967):
       Aug. 7: Considered and passed House.
       Oct. 12: Considered and passed Senate, amended.
       Nov. 28: Senate agreed to conference report.
       Nov. 29: House agreed to conference report.

[Figure 11—Copy of Act which became a law without approval of the President]

Public Law 93-190
93rd Congress, S. 2641
December 18, 1973

An Act

To confer jurisdiction upon the district court of the United States of certain civil actions brought by the Senate Select Committee on Presidential Campaign Activities, and for other purposes.

Be it enacted by the Senate and House of Representatives of the United States of America in Congress assembled, That (a) the District Court of the United States for the District of Columbia shall have original jurisdiction, without regard to the sum or value of the matter in controversy, of any civil action heretofore or hereafter brought by the Senate Select Committee on Presidential Campaign Activities, which was created on February 7, 1973, by Senate Resolution Numbered 60, to enforce or secure a declaration concerning the validity of any subpoena or order heretofore or hereafter issued by said Committee to the President or the Vice President or any other officer of the United States or any officer or employee of any department or agency of the United States to procure the production before the said Committee of any information, documents, taped recordings, or other materials relevant to matters the said Committee is authorized to investigate, and the said District Court shall have jurisdiction to enter any such judgment or decree in any such civil action as may be necessary or appropriate to enforce obedience to any such subpoena or order. *(U.S. District Court for the District of Columbia. Jurisdiction over civil actions brought by Senate Select Committee on Presidential Campaign Activities.)*

(b) The Senate Select Committee on Presidential Campaign Activities shall have authority to prosecute in its own name or in the name of the United States in the District Court of the United States for the District of Columbia any civil action heretofore or hereafter brought by said Committee to enforce or secure a declaration concerning the validity of any subpoena or order heretofore or hereafter issued by said Committee to the President or Vice President or any other officer of the United States or any officer or employee of any department of the United States to procure the production before the said Committee of any information, documents, taped recordings, or other materials relevant to the matters the Committee is authorized to investigate, and pray the said District Court to enter such judgment or decree in said civil action as may be necessary or appropriate to enforce any such subpoena or order. *(Prosecution authority.)* *87 STAT. 736* *87 STAT. 737*

(c) The Senate Select Committee on Presidential Campaign Activities may be represented by such attorneys as it may designate in any action prosecuted by said Committee under this Act. *(Attorney representation.)*

[Note by the Office of the Federal Register.—The foregoing Act, having been presented to the President of the United States on December 5, 1973, for his approval and not having been returned by him to the House of Congress in which it originated within the time prescribed by the Constitution of the United States, has become a law without his approval on December 18, 1973.]

LEGISLATIVE HISTORY:

HOUSE REPORT No. 93-661 (Comm. on the Judiciary).
CONGRESSIONAL RECORD, Vol. 119 (1973):
    Nov. 9, considered and passed Senate.
    Dec. 3, considered and passed House.
WEEKLY COMPILATION OF PRESIDENTIAL DOCUMENTS, Vol. 9 No. 51:
    Dec. 17, Presidential statement.

[Figure 12—Endorsements on Act which became a law after Presidential veto]

Public Law 93–148
November 7, 1973
93rd Congress, H. J. Res. 542

CARL ALBERT
Speaker of the House of Representatives.

JAMES O. EASTLAND
President of the Senate pro tempore.

IN THE HOUSE OF REPRESENTATIVES, U.S.,
November 7, 1973.

The House of Representatives having proceeded to reconsider the resolution (H. J. Res. 542) entitled "Joint resolution concerning the war powers of Congress and the President", returned by the President of the United States with his objections, to the House of Representatives, in which it originated, it was

Resolved, That the said resolution pass, two-thirds of the House of Representatives agreeing to pass the same.

Attest:

W. PAT JENNINGS
Clerk.

I certify that this Joint Resolution originated in the House of Representatives.

W. PAT JENNINGS
Clerk.

IN THE SENATE OF THE UNITED STATES
November 7, 1973.

The Senate having proceeded to reconsider the joint resolution (H. J. Res. 542) entitled "Joint resolution concerning the war powers of Congress and the President", returned by the President of the United States with his objections to the House of Representatives, in which it originated, it was

Resolved, That the said joint resolution pass, two-thirds of the Senators present having voted in the affirmative.

Attest:

FRANCIS R. VALEO
Secretary.

O